ROOT
TO
BLOOM

A MODERN GUIDE TO
WHOLE PLANT USE

HARVEST • COOK • PRESERVE • HEAL

ROOT TO BLOOM

A MODERN GUIDE TO WHOLE PLANT USE

HARVEST • COOK • PRESERVE • HEAL

Mat Pember & Jocelyn Cross

Hardie Grant

BOOKS

Edible parts of a plant

ROOT   STEM   LEAF

FLOWER 🌼   FRUIT 🍎   SEED

To think of coriander as a leaf is to think of a pig as bacon; it's only one of its many parts. This Homer Simpson form of tunnel vision (mmm, bacon) means we miss out on all the other delicious parts of plants that have only recently come to be regarded as waste. We are growing lots of perfectly edible food, then wasting most of it. Most disturbingly, the practice is so ingrained in us, that we are doing it in our gardens too.

Our perspective of what is food and what is waste is perhaps a by-product of a farming industry that for too long has been striving for efficiency in business rather than the efficient use of our resources. Plants that are grown exclusively for their fruit, foliage or seeds typically have many more edible parts. There are some exceptions, such as the nightshade family, which has poisonous flowers and foliage, but most plants, be it coriander, dill, peas or nasturtiums, are full of food, from the root all the way to the bloom.

As we understand more about the earth's limited resources, we must also revaluate our notion of resourcefulness. Resourcefulness has always been the cornerstone of our evolution. It is not a new idea. Recycling and composting, for example, are essential practices that have been around since the caveman killed his first beast, ate it almost entirely, made a coat out of the skin, used its bones for jewellery, then fed the rest to livestock and vultures who, in turn, fertilised his sprawling veggie patch.

From the wild greens that then flourished would have come edible flowers, too.

From this, came nose-to-tail eating, and it remains prevalent in almost every culture. It is standard practice among the Italian members of my family and, even though the 'Australian' half may seem out of touch, their Scottish ancestors certainly feasted on an offal-rich haggis or two. Recently, there has been a revival of nose-to-tail eating in the restaurant world, and it is often marketed as something new and sustainable. However, using the whole animal is an age-old concept, and the same can be said for using all parts of an edible plant.

When it comes to fruit, vegetables and herbs, we desperately need to revise our perspective of edibility. Both growers and consumers have become stuck on the idea that food is what we get at the supermarket, which is to say it is limited and uniform. Apparently it has to be, because we dump almost as much food as we eat because it is too long or too short, too skinny or too fat; in fact, too

anything other than perfect. And what about the other parts of these plants? The wasted bits that are perfectly edible but aren't valued by modern society? So many edible parts of common plants are needlessly discarded.

It is easy to become focused on the primary growth of our plants at the expense of everything else, but, as growers and consumers, it only takes a small aperture in our thinking to open up a world of culinary possibilities. For this reason, we want to bring back root-to-bloom eating.

Plants have so much to offer – all the way from the root to the bloom. Coriander, for example, is a completely edible plant. While we tend to favour its leaf foliage, it also produces sweet and pungent flowers, powerful-tasting stems and root matter and, of course, sought-after seeds, which are one of the most versatile spices in the pantry.

Most plants present an opportunity to harvest before and after their primary growth, which means we needn't wait months to enjoy the spoils of our labour.

It also means that even if we fail to grow that trophy pumpkin, the rest of the plant has not gone to waste. By enjoying the whole plant, we experience a whole new spectrum of flavour and texture that would otherwise end up in the compost bin.

The concept of root-to-bloom eating is something we continually strive to live by. Similar to the public consciousness of wasting unwanted parts of an animal in favour of more desirable cuts, we can't stand to see edible parts of a plant going to waste. More than that, we want to celebrate the sense of connection that growing and eating all parts of a plant gives us.

Exploring other parts of a plant is like peeling back layers from an onion; it's revealing. And while root-to-bloom eating isn't anything new, we think it should make a comeback, because when a plant and a gardener go to so much effort to grow something together, no part of it should be wasted.

ROOTS & SHOOTS

Root vegetables and rhizomes are some of our oldest and most nutritious cultivated vegetables. Their use dates back 8,000 years or more, both for culinary and medicinal purposes. The use of some varieties, such as beetroot and turmeric, has even diversified beyond food and medicine to being used for natural fabric dyes.

As with many other vegetables, various root vegetables have been identified as aphrodisiacs throughout history. The Greek name for carrot, *philtron*, means love charm, and beetroot derives its colour from a compound called betalain, which helps our body create sex hormones.

Growing underground, root vegetables and rhizomes have the most immediate access to the soil's nutrients. Root vegetables prefer cooler soils that help to convert their starches into sugars, while rhizomes prefer consistent warmth, otherwise lying dormant in cold conditions. Like a hibernating bear with only a few reserves in its belly, rhizomes have tough cellular walls and a powerful build-up of starches, which they use as fuel to help get them through the cool season.

Although the root is the ultimate prize, the foliage of just about every root vegetable and rhizome is edible too. Beetroot greens are commonly used in salads and are nutritionally comparable to kale and silverbeet. Carrot greens are tender and palatable and make a good substitute for parsley, while the foliage of ginger and turmeric is more plentiful than the rhizome itself.

Ginger leaves, for example, have a peppery flavour that is milder than the rhizome but more prolific, providing extra produce to cook with as the ginger root develops below. It also has the highest anti-cancer effect as stated by the United States National Cancer Institute.

CARROT

Daucus carota

Carrots were originally derived from Queen Anne's Lace,
a wild-growing weed with a white taproot that is becoming
increasingly popular for its own culinary value.

Although most of us would recognise carrots as orange, they come in a diverse range of natural colours that would outdo your favourite floral summer dress, from deep purple, to red, white and yellow. It was the Dutch who first domesticated carrots as sweeter, less fibrous roots and, over the years, carrots have been selectively bred to be more palatable.

Generally, the deeper the colour of the root the more nutritious it will be, and carrots are at their most colourful when young and freshly picked. While most vegetables are more nutritious when eaten raw, carrots need to be cooked to unlock their full potential. This is because they have tough cellular walls that are only broken down by cooking, making it easier for us to absorb their nutrients.

During World War Two, the British government encouraged people to eat carrots to improve their night vision so they could better observe and protect their new radar technology. Even though this was dispelled at the time as mere propaganda, carrots do carry a heavy dose of vitamin A, which helps improve eye health. The pigments that give carrots their colour help to reduce macular degeneration and improve eye function.

Aside from the root, the foliage is a much-wasted part that can be used instead of parsley as a garnish, or for greens in a stir-fry. While all parts of the stem are edible, the younger foliage tips are the most delicate and palatable. The flowering heads of the plant, which form in an upside-down umbrella shape, can also be eaten alongside the dried seeds, which can be used as a spice.

Nutritional value

Can help to balance intestinal gas, prevent constipation and treat indigestion. Carrots are also thought to improve skin health and contain potassium and antioxidants.

Origin

Afghanistan

Favourite variety

Any variety that is slightly odd-shaped or coloured. Chantenay is a stumpy, smooth-skinned variety that is particularly sweet and rich in colour.

Seasonality / In the garden

The carrot is a cooler-season vegetable that is most comfortable in soils below 20°C (68°F). Growing carrots in the warmer months often results in prolific foliage and flower growth, which can be trimmed and used in moderation so as not to affect the root development.

The key to growing straight carrots is even moisture and nutrition, which is easier to distribute in medium-density soils. Compacted soils will inhibit root growth, while soils that are too friable tend to make the roots chase food and water like a wild coyote.

Pickled radish seed pods

Makes 1 x 550 ml (18½ fl oz) jar

Radishes left to seed in-ground will produce an abundance of seeded green pods, which can be used to make this simple pickle. As the pods tend to become woody with age, it's imperative to catch them young when they are sharp and still crunchy. While all pickles are great on their own for snacking, they match well as a side dish to barbecued meats and add a surprising bite at the end of your Bloody (or Virgin) Mary.

100 g (3½ oz/2 cups) green radish seed pods, cleaned

Pickling liquid
125 ml (4 fl oz/½ cup) rice vinegar
125 ml (4 fl oz/½ cup) white-wine vinegar
115 g (4 oz/½ cup) caster (superfine) sugar
½ tablespoon salt

For the pickling liquid, combine all the ingredients in a small saucepan with 250 ml (8½ fl oz/1 cup) water and bring to a simmer over medium heat. Stir until the sugar and salt have dissolved, then remove from the heat and leave to cool.
  Pack the pods into a sterilised glass jar (see below), then pour over the pickling liquid until the pods are completely submerged.
  Store in a cool, dry place for 1 week, then enjoy. Once opened, they will keep for up to 2 months in the refrigerator.

Carrot frond chimichurri

Makes 250 ml (8½ fl oz/1 cup)

Chimichurri is a South American uncooked green (verde) or red (rojo) sauce, and is as popular a condiment there as tomato sauce is here. Coriander and parsley usually make up the bulk of the ingredients, but here we have substituted the herbs with carrot fronds, which give the sauce an earthier, more subtle green edge.

90 g (3 oz/3 cups) carrot fronds, finely chopped
125 ml (4 fl oz/½ cup) olive oil
¼ teaspoon chilli flakes
50 g (1¾ oz/⅓ cup) finely chopped shallot or
  red onion
3 garlic cloves, finely chopped or crushed
2 tablespoons white-wine vinegar
1–2 tablespoons freshly squeezed lime juice
salt and pepper, to taste

Combine all the ingredients in a small bowl and season to taste. Leave to rest for 30 minutes to 1 hour to allow the flavours to develop.
  Serve over grilled meat or fish.

Sterilising glass jars & bottles

Many of the recipes in this book can be stored in bottles or jars. To keep them tasting fresh and free of any contaminants, it's important to sterilise any glass bottles or jars before use. To do this, thoroughly wash the bottles and lids in hot soapy water. Place on a baking tray, mouths facing up, and leave in a very low oven until completely dry.

Carrot fronds replace the coriander (cilantro) and parsley in our take on a Chimichurri (left).

RADISH

Raphanus sativas

Egyptians were cultivating radishes by 2,780 BC, and these small vegetables are thought to have fuelled the slave labour that built the pyramids. The first radish was black-skinned but, over time, they have evolved into a diverse range of shapes and colours, from the tiny Cherry Belle to the giant daikon. Easy to grow from seed and quick to mature (although the daikon can take over 3 months), they are a small-space, home-grown favourite.

————————

The roots are typically served raw or pickled and, in the West, they are often used as an appetiser to a main meal. In Asian culture, radishes follow large, fatty banquets to aid digestion. An old folk medicine recommends consuming radishes for a number of days on an empty stomach to help pass kidney stones.

————————

In the garden, radishes are the ultimate confidence booster, given their high rate of germination and growth, which means slugs and snails are often too slow to do any real damage.

As they grow, you can harvest the leaves, which can be sautéed or used fresh in salads. The younger growth is most palatable, while older leaves tend to be coarse and spicy.

Nutritional value

Rich source of folic acid, potassium, vitamin B, magnesium, copper and calcium. Stimulates appetite and aids digestion. They also have antibacterial and antifungal qualities.

Origin

Europe

Favourite variety

Cherry Belle, a smooth, red-skinned variety that is quick to mature and has palatable leaf foliage.

Seasonality / In the garden

Radish is the least fussy of all root vegetables and, while it prefers to grow during the cooler months, it will tolerate plenty of sun and warmth too. Summer tends to make the roots spicier than those grown in the winter, however they mature more quickly and both roots and leaf foliage is bountiful. Leaving the plants in-ground under the stress of heat will cause them to shoot seed heads and sprout edible flowers that have a mild peppery flavour.

HORSERADISH

Armoracia lapathifolia

It is said that the Delphic oracle told Apollo 'the radish is worth its weight in lead, the beet its weight in silver and the horseradish its weight in gold'. Not surprisingly, horseradish has been prized for its medicinal and culinary uses for thousands of years. The ancient Greeks used it as a salve for lower back pain, while English inn-keepers made it into a cordial to revive exhausted travellers.

The term for radish originated with the German word *meetrettich*, meaning sea radish, as it was found growing wild in coastal areas. The English then adopted the name mareradish (mare the mispronunciation of meer), until finally settling on horseradish: 'horse' denoting the large size and coarseness of the root.

Horseradish paste is made by grating or grinding the freshly harvested roots of the plant. As the cells of the root are broken, isothiocyanates are released. This volatile compound is what generates the horseradish's notorious 'heat' when oxidised by air and saliva. Vinegar stops this reaction and stabilises the flavour, so for a milder horseradish paste, add vinegar immediately after grating the root.

Most of the wasabi paste you get with your takeaway sushi is really just horseradish paste mixed with food colouring. It is only in some very fine-dining Japanese restaurants that you will find authentic wasabi paste made from the wasabi plant (a member of the mustard family). Like horseradish, wasabi grows wild along waterways.

Although the main prize of horseradish is its root, like all members of the mustard family, the leaves and flowers of the plant can be used in salads.

The foliage is best used when it is younger and more palatable; leaves left too long are extremely tough, fibrous and overbearing.

Nutritional value

It is not surprising that a plant as spicy as horseradish is packed with nutrients. It has antibacterial properties and also acts as a diuretic, treating kidney stones and increasing perspiration and circulation. Its heating properties help cut through mucus and can be used as a lo-fi sinus-clearing remedy.

Origin

Central Europe

Favourite variety

Bohemian Giant, which has fleshy roots and smooth leaf foliage.

Seasonality/In the garden

Horseradish can be grown from seedling or root stock and, being a member of the mustard family, it grows best during the cooler months. The leaf foliage is more palatable and tender when young. Left too long in-ground, it can become overwhelmingly hot and fibrous. The roots develop their pungency when left to mature in cool soil, so if seeking a spicy harvest, allow to develop during the cooler months of the year.

Roots and shoots chicken curry

Serves 4

There is something special about creating your very own fresh curry paste with the leftover produce in the veggie garden.

This curry is inspired by an Elizabeth David recipe I found in an old box set of Penguin Asian Cookbooks from the 1970s. I came across it 15 to 20 years ago when I was searching for an authentic Indian curry that I could make from scratch. The original recipe calls for dried herbs and spices, but I have adapted this recipe to include many of our fresh root-to-bloom ingredients for extra zest and heat. The yoghurt base gives this curry a lovely mellow finish.

2 large onions, finely diced
4 garlic cloves (and a handful of garlic scapes if you
   have them)
5 cm (2 in) piece of turmeric, peeled and chopped
5 cm (2 in) piece of ginger, peeled and chopped
small handful of finely chopped ginger and
   turmeric leaves
2 teaspoons fresh green coriander seeds (if you don't
   have fresh, use 1 tablespoon dried coriander seeds)
1 teaspoon cumin seeds
1 red chilli, chopped
1 teaspoon paprika
100 ml (3½ fl oz) olive oil or ghee
2 kaffir lime leaves
1 small cinnamon stick
1 green cardamom pod
1 kg (2 lb 3 oz) free-range chicken thighs, cut into
   2 cm (¾ in) strips
120 ml (4 fl oz) natural yoghurt
sea salt, to taste
basmati rice, to serve
coriander (cilantro) leaves, to garnish

In a pestle and mortar, grind one of the onions with the garlic, turmeric and ginger (and their leaves), coriander seeds, cumin seeds, chilli and paprika to form a paste. Heat the oil in a large frying pan over high heat and fry the other onion until golden. Reduce the heat to medium and add the kaffir lime leaves, cinnamon stick and cardamom and fry for another 1–2 minutes until the kaffir leaves are crisp.

Add the paste, a pinch of salt and the chicken pieces and fry for 3–5 minutes. Add the yoghurt, then briefly bring the curry to the boil before lowering the heat to a simmer. Cover and simmer gently to reduce the sauce (this will take about 5 minutes). Once the curry has reduced, remove the lid and simmer until it becomes a beautiful, rich brown colour.

Serve with basmati rice and garnish with fresh coriander leaves.

Horseradish cream

Makes 200 ml (7 fl oz)

½ fresh horseradish root
75 ml (2½ fl oz) thick (double/heavy) cream
75 ml (2½ fl oz) crème fraîche
2 teaspoons white-wine vinegar
½ teaspoon English mustard
sea salt, ground white pepper and caster (superfine)
   sugar, to taste

Wash, peel and finely grate the horseradish root; you will need 2–3 tablespoons of grated horseradish.

Combine the grated horseradish, cream, crème fraîche, vinegar and mustard in a bowl and leave to macerate for a few hours to allow the strength of the horseradish to develop. Season to taste with salt, pepper and a little sugar.

GINGER/TURMERIC

Zingiber officinale/Curcuma longa

Ginger and turmeric are rhizomes native to India that grow best in tropical and subtropical regions. Ginger is second only to salt as a condiment in Asian cooking, and is found in roughly half of all Chinese and Indian (Ayurvedic) medicine prescriptions. In Ayurvedic medicine, ginger is known as *vishwabhesaj* or 'universal medicine'. Turmeric, though not as revered in either a medicinal or culinary sense, is still held in high esteem. It is an essential ingredient in Indian cooking and is used as a natural food colouring; Buddhist monks use it for dyeing their robes.

The roots of both plants are typically ground to a powder or used fresh. Ginger root is also pickled and candied, and used as a flavouring to make beer, while turmeric root is a powerful food and fabric dye.

Although both are often peeled for cooking, unless they are being dried or candied, peeling the nutritious skin is not necessary. While you are waiting to harvest the root, the palm-like leaves of both plants can be used as milder substitutes for the root itself.

Ginger stems are a great vegetable in their own right and can be used in stir-fries or steamed alone as a spicy accompaniment to fish and pork dishes. When harvesting the leaves or stems, be sure to pick at ground level. This allows the rhizome – and the rest of the plant – to quickly recover and maintain growth.

Nutritional value

Both are known to stimulate digestion and help respiration, as well as being anti-inflammatory and antibacterial. Ginger has been widely used in the treatment of cold and flu symptoms for thousands of years, as well as relieving headaches and menstrual pain. Turmeric can help young children assimilate protein, so can be combined with milk when they are young. It is also used topically in the treatment of cold sores.

Origin

India

Favourite variety

Common ginger and Common turmeric.

Seasonality/In the garden

Both ginger and turmeric thrive best in subtropical and tropical regions. If you happen to live in a cooler area, try growing in a hot and protected part of your garden so that the plant gets maximum access to sunlight. Even better, grow it in a pot and move it around. Ginger and turmeric are sown from sprouting rhizomes in early spring. The time to harvest and divide the plants is late autumn, but you will be able to pick and use the leaf foliage throughout the growing season.

YARROW

Achillea millefolium

Yarrow is a wildflower and a member of the sunflower family.
It is closely related to chamomile and is seen as a symbol of good luck
in Chinese culture. The genus name for yarrow, *achillea*, is derived
from the mythical Greek character, Achilles, who supposedly
carried it with his army to treat battle wounds. Its leaves, intricately
woven and fern-like in appearance, have antiseptic properties
and, when layered over a wound, will help clot the blood
and prevent infection.

In the Middle Ages, yarrow made up part of a herbal mixture known as gruit, which was used to flavour beer before the use of hops. It has also been used in traditional Native American medicine. The Navajo tribe considered it a 'life medicine' and chewed it for toothaches as well as applying it to the eardrum to help cure earaches. The Miwok in California used the plant as a head-cold remedy.

While not commonly consumed today, in the seventeenth century, yarrow foliage was eaten as a popular leafy green, prepared and consumed much like spinach. Its flavour is bittersweet, making it a good substitute for tarragon.

Its real value in the vegetable garden is as a companion plant that helps to attract beneficial insects, both to curb pests and disease and help pollinate flowers into fruits. As a perennial plant, it will provide a number of years of good service in your garden.

Nutritional value

Yarrow contains a natural antiseptic that will help prevent skin infections, but it has also been used to treat headaches and relieve the symptoms of cold and flu. It is found to be useful in the treatment of mastitis, a breast infection of the nipple common among new nursing mothers.

Origin

Native to eastern Europe and western Asia.

Favourite variety

Red, for its rich red flower and matted, fern-like foliage.

Seasonality/In the garden

Yarrow is a perennial, herbaceous plant that is highly prized in the garden for its companionship, attracting beneficial insects such as ladybirds and hoverflies to help curb pests. Its bright, tall flowers that bloom throughout late spring and summer also attract pollinators such as bees. Each plant will shoot a number of tall, slender stem heads, with compact, fern-like foliage. When harvesting foliage as leafy greens, pick from the lower parts of the plant and work your way up. The younger, softer foliage will be more tender and less peppery than foliage that has been left to overcook on the stem.

The yarrow's fern-like foliage can be used as a leafy herb to substitute tarragon, or the entire plant can be steeped to make a bitter tea that is delicious mixed with some honey.

BEETROOT

Beta vulgaris

There is little that beetroot can't do. Its foliage is a superfood rich in vitamins and minerals – belonging to the same family as silverbeet – and its deep purple root can be eaten boiled, steamed, pickled or grated fresh. It is also a powerful fabric and food dye, and the pigment that gives beetroot its colour (called betalain) is responsible for the creation of our sex hormones. This might explain why Ancient Romans considered it an aphrodisiac.

Beetroot has the highest sugar content of all vegetables; so much so that the sugar beet, which is directly related to the common red beetroot, accounts for one-third of the world's sugar production. In case you're interested, the remaining production comes from sugarcane and corn.

If you want to gauge your iron levels without a trip to the doctor, try eating a couple of Bull's Blood beetroots (which are extremely high in betalain) and wait to see how it affects your digestive system. Passing pink urine may indicate an iron deficiency, whereas dark red stools suggest a normal level of iron.

When growing beetroot, allow the roots to mature in cool soil. This allows the conversion of starches into sugars and ensures the beetroot's sweetness. Fresh roots don't store particularly well, so only harvest as required and be sure to harvest the plants' foliage in moderation so as not to impact root development.

Nutritional value

Beetroot greens are an excellent source of vitamins A, C and K and folic acid, and contain more calcium and iron than the roots. Both are good sources of dietary fibre and are high in potassium, magnesium, copper and boron, which is critical for the production of sex hormones. The pigment that colours beetroot, known as betalain, is an anti-carcinogen.

Origin

Mediterranean

Favourite variety

Cream rings, for its layered white and pink flesh that, when cut, looks like cream rings.

Seasonality / In the garden

Beetroot is best grown during the cool season, but it will grow at any time of the year. Summer is the most prolific growing period for beetroot greens, which are probably the most palatable of all root vegetables. To get the most out of a single plant, be sure to harvest foliage evenly from all plants, as excessive foliage harvest will limit a plant's ability to develop the root.

Organic beetroot fabric dye

I've often dyed my clothes by accident, but here is a more purposeful approach using the powerful pigments of the beetroot. Some beetroot will dye better than others, and I prefer to use Bull's Blood for their deep colour. The outcome also hinges on the origin of your fabric. This dye works better for animal-based textiles like wool rather than plant-based ones, imparting a soft, earthy peach tone to your fabric.

Cut 3–4 beetroot into chunks (wear gloves if you want to avoid looks of suspicion). Place in a large enamel pot, fill with water and bring to the boil, then reduce the heat and simmer for an hour or so. At this point, the water will be a deep red, so remove the chunks from the pot.

Bring the beetroot dye back to a simmer, add your fabric or yarn and simmer for another hour.

Remove the pot from the heat and leave the fabric to sit in the water for another 2 hours to soak in the colour before draining and drying the fabric.

Beetroot pasta
Serves 4

500 g (1 lb 2 oz) tipo 00 flour, plus extra for dusting
3 large organic, free-range eggs
120 g (4½ oz) cooked, peeled and puréed beetroot
semolina, for dusting

Empty the flour onto a clean work surface and create a hole, or well, in the middle. In a small bowl, beat the eggs with a fork, then add the beetroot purée, mix and pour into the flour well. Using your hands, gently work the flour in from the edges until completely combined. If the mixture feels too sticky, add a little more flour.

Dust your surface with a little more flour and knead the dough until elastic. Form it into a ball, then transfer to a clean, oiled bowl and cover with plastic wrap. Refrigerate for about 30 minutes before dividing the dough into four pieces and forming into balls.

Use a pasta maker to prepare your pasta sheets, beginning with the widest setting and rolling to the second-last setting on the roller. Fold your dough in half between each roll and dust generously with the semolina.

Feed the pasta through the spaghetti or fettucine setting on the pasta maker, or hand-cut pappardelle or ravioli.

A note about drying pasta
Pasta is best enjoyed fresh and it only takes a few minutes to cook. If you double the recipe, you can dry the rest and you'll have home-made pasta for next time.

First, cut the pasta into the shape you want, dust well with semolina and dry it on a well-floured surface (baking paper or a wire rack is ideal) so it doesn't stick. Alternatively, hang spaghetti and pappardelle on a wooden coathanger or clean broom suspended between two chairs. Allow to dry for 1–2 days until completely dry. (The pasta should snap in your hand when properly dried.)

Dried pasta can be stored in an airtight container for up to 2 months. Cook for 8–10 minutes in boiling salted water.

Beetroot pasta (left) has a subtle, earthy flavour that pairs well with strong cheeses and pungent herbs.

SWEET POTATO

Ipomoea batatas

Despite its name, the sweet potato is not that closely related
to the regular potato or its assumed cousin, the yam. Likewise,
it is not a member of the poisonous nightshade family, which
is another common misconception. Instead, it is a bindweed;
a member of the morning glory family that includes
approximately 1,000 fast-growing, flowering vines.

Sweet potatoes grow wild throughout the tropical and subtropical forests of Central America, and prefer a relatively stable air temperature of approximately 24°C (75°F). In these areas, they are a year-round perennial plant with vigorous vine growth that produces long, tapered tubers. The skin and flesh of the tuber comes in a variety of colours, from the more common orange and purple, to yellow, white and pink. Although it is the tuber that is most commonly consumed, the leaves are edible too and, due to their prolific nature, should be more valued as a willing and able substitute for spinach.

Cuttings from a sweet potato vine are often grown as ornamental indoor plants, and roots will rapidly form from the cutting when placed in water and allowed to grow in good light and a consistent temperature. Its rapid growth is fuelled by toxic ammonia and nitrates – the waste product of aquatic life – and so, the sweet potato vine is ideal for use in home aquariums or hydroponic systems.

Nutritional value

Regarded as one of the most nutrient-dense vegetables, sweet potato is high in vitamins A and C, and is a very good source of antioxidants, particularly the varieties with the darker orange flesh.

Origin

Central America, where they grow wild. There are remnants of the vegetable dating as far back as 8,000 BC.

Favourite variety

Japanese, which has a red/purple skin and sweet white flesh that turns orange when baked.

Seasonality / In the garden

A perennial in warmer, more tropical regions, sweet potato can be grown as an annual in more temperate zones where it will be intolerant to cold conditions. For this reason, it should be planted from a cutting in late spring and, depending on the variety, will produce tubers any time from 2–6 months after it enters the garden. While all leaves from the plant can be harvested, the vine's tips are the most tender and flavoursome, and clipping these will also help swell the tubers underground. Late in the season, take some cuttings indoors and propagate these directly into water. They can be maintained through the winter as an indoor plant, ready for the following warm season.

The foliage of the sweet potato can be used as a substitute for spinach and is best wilted through dishes.

ONION

Allium cepa

The Ancient Egyptians revered the onion, considering its spherical shape and many layers as a symbol of eternal life; so much so, that it was used in traditional burials. It was also highly regarded by other ancient cultures, with documents suggesting that Greek athletes ate it in large quantities, both raw and in juice form, and rubbed it on themselves to strengthen their bodies before competition.

Onions can be both sweet and spicy, and different varieties will suit different purposes. They can be pickled and stewed into jams, eaten raw in salads or, most commonly, fried as a base for a dish. True onion connoisseurs will have favoured varieties depending on how they plan to consume them and, with so many varieties available, growing onions at home is the best way to explore their flavours.

The sulphurous acid that makes you cry when cutting an onion is released when the onion's cell walls are broken. This is more pronounced in older, spicier onions, so younger, sweeter bulbs are easier (and less tear-inducing) to chop. You can also cut onions under running water or burn a candle next to your chopping board so the flame consumes the sulphur as it's released.

The onion and its relatives in the allium family are prohibited from yogic diets because they apparently increase sexual appetite. However, as an avid consumer of pickled onions and user of regular onion in my daily diet, I notice little shift in my sexual desire, or luck for that matter.

Nutritional value

In Indian, or Ayurvedic, medicine the onion has been used as a diuretic to aid digestion and ease the joints. Onions have antibacterial and anti-inflammatory properties and are high in antioxidants, making them a common ingredient in home cold remedies.

Origin

Central Asia, and is one of our oldest cultivated vegetables.

Favourite variety

French shallots, for their flavoursome greens and small, complex multi-bulbed heads.

Seasonality/In the garden

All members of the allium family need exposure to cool soil conditions in order to mature. The onion enjoys a prolonged stay in the veggie patch that begins in early autumn and concludes sometime in spring. Onion greens, or scapes, as they are commonly referred to, can be picked early on in the growing process and used as a substitute for spring onions. Bulbs typically signal they are ready once the foliage begins to brown off and die back. Allowing them to overcook in-ground will create long, ridged seed heads followed by pungent white flowers. These flowers have a more delicate onion flavour than the bulb or scapes.

The sweet-tasting white flower clusters of the onion plant are its crowning culinary glory. Break apart the dense heads and scatter the flowers over your favourite risotto.

MEDICINAL

We have always relied on plants to treat illness and soothe aches and pains. In fact, most cultures still do. Although modern medicine has refined natural ingredients into dusty white pills, we can't forget that most of our important medicines are derived from plants. Nature truly is the master chemist and possesses all the keys for unlocking good health.

At the core of edible plants are properties that make them beneficial to our health and keep our systems in check, making us more immune to illness and disease. We all know how much fruit and veg' we need to maintain good health, but we have lost touch with the medicinal arsenal of plant life. Plants contain over 12,000 known active compounds that impact human biological function and their use for the treatment of human ailments is an ancient and proven science.

Plants have always been revered for their powers; some scientific and others more mystical. The Egyptians, for one, considered the onion to be a symbol of the universe. They believed its skins represented the layers of the nether world and heaven, and they even took their oath on an onion and presented them as sacrificial offerings to their gods.

Stories of Egyptian onion sacrifice may intensify skepticism around plants as medicine but, for us, it only highlights the complex nature of plants and their value, which is not fully understood or appreciated.

How can a civilisation be responsible for one of the greatest feats of human engineering and yet revere the humble onion as a symbol of the universe? Surely there must be more to the onion than being merely a base for good soup?

Like root-to-bloom eating, medicinal plant use is not something new. It is not a new-age idea, nor is it a sub-culture practice reserved only for hippies. To capture the indisputable healing powers of plants, modern medicine isolates singular compounds and synthesises them for commercial use. These days, there is a pill for everything, but let's not forget the healing powers and value of our plants.

Basil

(Oiumum basilicum)

The luscious and aromatic leaves of the basil plant may hit the spot torn over your margarita pizza or fresh burrata, but did you know it also has proven medicinal benefits? Upheld by modern pharmacology, basil is known to relieve flatulence, and a tea made from its leaves is taken for nausea, painful gas and dysentery.

Basil-peppercorn chai tea (Tulshicha Chaha)
Makes 500 ml (17 fl oz/2 cups)

Used in Ayurvedic medicine, this sacred tea helps reduce fever.

1 bunch basil leaves
2 teaspoons black peppercorns
3 tablespoons black tea leaves
500 ml (17 fl oz/2 cups) full-cream (whole) milk
45 g (1½ oz/¼ cup, firmly packed) light brown sugar

Combine the basil leaves and peppercorns in a saucepan and crush using the back of a spoon. Add 1.5 litres (52 fl oz/6 cups) water and bring to the boil. Reduce the heat to medium–low, partially cover the pan with a lid, and simmer gently for 10 minutes.
  Remove from the heat, add the tea leaves and leave to infuse for 5 minutes. Add the milk and sugar, then bring back to a simmer over medium–low heat, whisking until the sugar has dissolved.
  To serve, strain through a fine-mesh sieve into mugs and discard the solids.

Elderberry

(Sambucus nigra)

Elderberries possess antiviral properties that have been shown to treat colds and flu. A syrup made from the berry can be used as a remedy for coughs, and a tea made from the flowers acts as a mild laxative or diuretic. Elderflower water is still used today (and sold commercially) as a skin lotion.

Elderberry cough medicine
Makes 500 ml (17 fl oz/2 cups)

100 g (3½ oz/²/₃ cup) dried elderberries
2 tablespoons freshly chopped ginger
1 teaspoon ground cinnamon
½ teaspoon whole cloves
350 g (12½ oz/1 cup) raw honey

Combine the elderberries, ginger, cinnamon and cloves in a saucepan with 875 ml (29½ fl oz/3½ cups) water. Bring to the boil, then reduce the heat to medium, cover and simmer for 45–60 minutes. Set aside to cool.
  Strain the liquid through a fine-mesh sieve into a clean bowl, discarding the solids. Once the liquid has cooled and feels lukewarm, add the honey and stir well to dissolve.
  Pour the cough syrup into a sterilised glass jar or bottle (see page 14) and store in the refrigerator for up to 2 months.

Fennel

(Foeniculum vulgare)

Today, herbalists still recommend a tea made from crushed fennel seeds for indigestion and cramps (also as an eyewash). In Ancient Rome, an extract from the root was even prescribed as a treatment for cataracts.

Fennel seed digestive tea
Makes 250 ml (8½ fl oz/1 cup)

Fennel seeds are especially high in the essential oils that help ease flatulence, so they make an excellent tea to stimulate digestion.

Lightly crush 1½ teaspoons fennel seeds with the back of a spoon, then place them in a mesh tea strainer in a cup. Pour over 250 ml (8½ fl oz/1 cup) boiling water and allow to infuse for 5–7 minutes before drinking.

Horseradish

(Armoracia rusticana)

This well-known culinary herb is also used as a diuretic, digestive stimulant (diaphoretic) and as a snuff for clearing clogged nasal passages. In permaculture, a natural fungicide can be prepared from the horseradish leaves (see page 63).

Horseradish snuff for nasal congestion

This simple preparation encourages blocked mucus to loosen and drain, relieving sinus pain and pressure.

Place ¼ teaspoon grated fresh horseradish in your mouth and hold it, without chewing, for about 30 seconds or until the flavour subsides. Repeat 2–3 times per day when feeling congested.

Nasturtium

(Trapaeoleum)

Nasturtiums have been used in herbal medicine for hundreds of years for their antiseptic and expectorant qualities. They are also good for chest colds and help to promote the formation of new blood cells. The nasturtium variety *Trapaeoleum majus* is used in herbal medicine for respiratory and urinary tract infections.

Nasturtium leaf tea for chesty coughs
Serves 2

Place 2 teaspoons torn nasturtium leaves in a teapot and pour in 500 ml (17 fl oz/2 cups) boiling water. Cover and leave to infuse for 10 minutes, then strain through a fine-mesh sieve into mugs, discarding the solids.

Turmeric

(Curcuma longa)

Part of the ginger family, turmeric has been used as a stimulant, to treat eye infections, blood diseases and nasal passage inflammation.

The active ingredient in turmeric is curcumin and, interestingly, it is used in modern medicine for both cancer prevention and treatment. Curcumin has anti-proliferative properties, which inhibit the spread of a wide variety of tumour cells and metastasis in-vitro by reducing cell activity and invasion.

Turmeric anti-inflammatory tea
Serves 2

2.5 cm (1 in) piece of turmeric, peeled and grated
honey and freshly squeezed lemon, to taste

Put the turmeric in a small saucepan with 500 ml (17 fl oz/2 cups) water and bring to a simmer over medium heat. Line a fine-mesh sieve with a piece of muslin (cheesecloth) and strain the tea into cups. Add lemon and honey to taste.

Tip: Finely chopped ginger will boost this drink's anti-inflammatory effect.

Turmeric anti-inflammatory cream
Makes 125 ml (4 fl oz/½ cup)

In Ayurvedic medicine, turmeric paste is often used to cleanse wounds and reduce inflammation.

Put 1 teaspoon ground turmeric in a small bowl and add 125 ml (4 fl oz/½ cup) warm water or sesame oil. Mix to a paste and apply to the affected area of skin.

Valerian

(Valeriana officinalis)

Valerian has long been considered a cure for epilepsy. In the sixteenth and seventeenth centuries, it was considered a sedative and an antispasmodic used to treat convulsions.

During World War One, it was used to treat shellshock and, during World War Two, was used during air raids to calm frightened citizens.

Today, the powdered rhizomes, or rootstock, of valerian are still widely used as a herbal sedative. Pharmacological studies have also validated its use as an antispasmodic for intestinal pains.

Home-made sleep potion
Makes 500 ml (17 fl oz/2 cups)

This tonic is best taken about 45 minutes before bed. Simply dissolve 10 drops in a little water or fruit juice to drink.

50 g (1¾ oz) dried passion flower
50 g (1¾ oz) dried valerian root
500 ml (17 fl oz/2 cups) vodka
  (50 per cent ABV)

Combine the dried herbs in a sterilised 500 ml (17 fl oz/2 cup) glass jar (see page 14) and pour over the vodka. Seal tightly and store in a cool, dark place away from direct sunlight.

Leave to macerate for 6 weeks, checking occasionally to see if you need to top up the vodka. The vodka will change colour over time.

Line a fine-mesh sieve with muslin (cheesecloth) and strain the vodka into sterilised amber glass dropper bottles for easy dosage. Store in the refrigerator for up to 1 year.

Olive leaf

(Olea europaea)

Today, olive leaf extract is widely available commercially, but for many centuries the fresh leaves of the olive tree were used in natural medicine. Olive leaves contain a treasure trove of compounds used to treat many conditions, from high blood pressure and diabetes, to obesity, Alzheimer's disease and heart disease. It's even known to improve brain function and burn fat, and studies have shown it prevents genetic damage and cancer growth.

Rates of cardiovascular disease and cancer are lowest in the Mediterranean regions, and this is attributed to their olive-rich diets. A clinical trial found that the Mediterranean diet improves cognitive function and reduces the risk of age-related cognitive diseases like dementia.

Olive leaf tincture
Makes 500 ml (17 fl oz/2 cups)

Making a tincture is an easy way to draw out the medicinal properties of the olive leaf and preserve them for long-term use. Alcohol stores best, but you can also use vinegar.

200 g (7 oz) fresh olive leaves
500 ml (17 fl oz/2 cups) vodka
  (80 per cent ABV)

Wash and finely chop the olive leaves, then place them in a sterilised 500 ml (17 fl oz/2 cup) glass jar (see page 14). Pour over the vodka and seal the jar tightly. Leave to macerate in a cool, dark place for approximately 4 weeks, shaking occasionally to ensure the leaves are evenly dispersed. Top up the vodka if required.

Strain through a fine-mesh sieve and store in sterilised glass dropper bottles for easy administration. Store in the refrigerator for up to 1 year.

CANCER & THE PLANT WORLD

Like all living things, both plants and humans are prone to diseases; some fatal and some treatable. Collar rot from overwatering and a lack of drainage may kill a plant, while powdery mildew can be easily treated by applying a fungicide. Chronic diseases, such as cardiovascular disease and cancer, continue to kill humans, either due to poor lifestyle choices, wonky genes or, in many cases, just bad luck.

While writing this book, I was delivered a breast cancer diagnosis and, in my case, it was probably a bit of bad luck (and possibly some wonky genes). After several surgeries to 'get rid' of the cancer, I'm now in the chair every few weeks having chemotherapy and, not surprisingly, it is our friends from the plant world that are helping me get better.

In the 1960s, the yew tree was discovered to have significant anti-cancer properties. The bark and needles from this eerily enormous conifer were collected to make one of my current-day chemotherapy drugs, Taxotere (Paclitaxel), putting a whole new spin on needles in your veins.

Fifty years on from this discovery, after the destructive harvesting of the yew tree for cancer treatments combined with pressure from environmentalists, Taxotere is now easily synthesised from the leaf extracts of the European Yew tree.

Globally, cancer is the second leading cause of death, overtaking AIDS, tuberculosis and malaria combined, and it is forecast to increase at a rate of millions over the next 15 years.

With such an epidemic on our hands, the science world is now turning to the plant world for a solution to control and treat the carcinogenic cell production that causes cancer.

Plants offer an enormous reservoir of natural chemicals that may provide us with numerous agents to fight cancer. Many of our common garden herbs are being studied in clinical trials to gain understanding of their potential to kill and prevent various cancers, and some of our root-to-bloom heroes, such as nigella, asparagus and turmeric have even been proven to have chemo-protective properties. Not only are we unleashing these plants' cytotoxic potential (the control of cancer through treatments like chemotherapy), but we are also looking to molecular management in the prevention of cancer.

STEMS & STALKS

Selective breeding of plant varieties for consumption has completely changed vegetables over time. Our focus on more palatable and uniformly shaped varieties has meant that all vegetables are now held to standards of colour and shape. We have come to recognise the tomato as red and perfectly round, and the carrot as orange, tapered and long. In fact, all vegetables now seem to be defined by a single variety.

Bitterness or astringency in our vegetables is another thing that we have bred out. Many put enjoying bitter flavours down to an acquired taste, but we believe it's a symptom of our senses becoming too sensitive to the taste of real food. The food we eat today is generally sweeter-tasting and more crowd pleasing than ever before. Perhaps it makes our vegetables more edible, and therefore more accessible, or it could mean breeding out varieties that are actually very good for us.

Take celery as a case in point. Before it was popularised as a vegetable in the eighteenth century, it was almost exclusively used for its medicinal properties and as a leaf herb. The stalk itself was very bitter so, over time, sweeter varieties were bred and the stems were blanched using soil or mulch to protect them from sunlight. Today, growers use ethylene gas to make the stalks sweeter.

Modern-day celery tastes very different to how it used to and, thanks to the commercial practice of gassing the stems, it is one of the most toxic vegetables on the shelf. The bitterness that can be found in your home-grown or organically grown varieties is a reminder of how the plant ought to taste.

CHIVE

Allium schoenoprasum

A perennial and compact herb, chives are a culinary staple, equally adored for their hollow, sweet onion-flavoured stems as for their clusters of purple flowers that typically appear in late spring and into summer. Chives are best used fresh as they lose their subtle flavour when overcooked or dried.

44

The rise of the edible flower movement has seen a notable increase in the use of chive flowers, which can often be found complementing both sweet and savoury dishes. To help promote flower heads, pick regularly and feed with a potash solution that will focus energy towards them. Common chives flower around late spring, but you'll have to wait for a smaller window in mid-autumn to catch the flowers of garlic chives.

As much as they are regarded for their produce, chives can also benefit the garden (and its visitors) on a number of levels. The plant provides masses of nectar for pollinators – in fact, it was listed in the top 10 for nectar-producing plants in a UK survey – and can be used to make an anti-fungal spray (see page 63) and a mild insect repellent.

Nutritional value

Dense in minerals, vitamins and antioxidants that assist with heart and bone health. Not as potent as garlic chives (that purportedly help male impotence due to kidney weakness), common chives are a mild tonic for blood circulation and benefit the digestive system.

Origin

Native to Asia and arctic Europe, chives have been around for more than 5,000 years, although they weren't actively cultivated until the Middle Ages. The botanical name is derived from Greek meaning 'reed-like leek'.

Favourite variety

Giant Siberian chives are similar to common chives, however much taller and stronger flavoured with large flower heads.

Seasonality / In the garden

Chives are a perennial herb that flower over a prolonged period in spring and summer. Much like mowing a lawn, clipping the tops of the stems will help promote new growth, so in order to keep production up, you'll need to harvest regularly. The same applies to the flowers where continually picking the buds frees up plant energy to produce new blooms.

The densely packed lilac blossoms are best broken apart and added to mashed potatoes. They impart a subtle, sweet chive flavour, but it's the highlight of colour that really makes the dish.

ASPARAGUS

Asparagus officinalis

Despite its mantle as one of the culinary heavyweights,
if there is one vegetable that needs an overhaul in our thinking,
it is the asparagus. Typically distinguished by colour – green,
purple or entirely white – or by width; the female varieties
produce slimmer crowns than the males.

If you too experience a form of tunnel vision when propositioned with a neatly wrapped bunch of asparagus, try growing it in your garden. Capturing the plant in its different stages of imperfection more closely mimics how it is found in the wild, and unlocks various culinary possibilities.

Harvesting early, when the crowns are delicately sweet, or late, once the plant has become a bush of fronds, provides an opportunity for different textures and tastes. Raw asparagus – how it was traditionally eaten many centuries ago – is the truest form of this vegetable, and is surprisingly sweet when compared to farmed produce.

Asparagus can be found in the wild in cooler climates where rhizomes will go dormant through the winter before shooting back up at the first signs of spring. Unlike parts of Europe and North America, wild asparagus is not often found growing wild in Australia. If you do happen across it, avoid picking from roadsides, which are typically sprayed to control weeds. Instead, focus on the borders of lush farmlands or unkempt creeks and riverbanks.

Most people will experience the 'asparagus odour' in their urine after eating the vegetable, and that is because asparagus contains asparagine, which is a diuretic for people that lack the gene to break it down. In case you were wondering, we are two of those people.

Nutritional value

Low in calories, asparagus is a good source of dietary fibre and calcium, as well as vitamin C, E and K. Vitamin K is responsible for helping the binding of calcium to bone and tissue. It reduces phlegm and mucus, while easing constipation and assisting liver function. It also helps to strengthen the immune system, as well as having anti-carcinogenic properties.

Origin

Native and wild to most of Europe. In fact, it makes up a recipe in a collection of Ancient Roman cookbooks: *Apicius third century AD de re coquinaria*, Book III, securing its place as one of the oldest-used vegetables.

Favourite variety

Precoce d'argenteuil is an old French heirloom with sweet-tasting stems and pale pink buds that turn white once cooked.

Seasonality/In the garden

Asparagus is one of the first vegetables to indicate that spring is upon us, and it will begin to spear from the ground as soil temperature improves. The first spears of spring will be too irresistible to refuse. Cut them with a sharp knife a few centimetres below the surface, then cover with soil to aid further production. Any spears you don't get to will begin to develop into thin, wispy fronds, which are just as sweet and more delicate than the stems. These are good to cut from until they become tough.

Celery salt

Makes approx. 100 g (3½ oz)

Celery salt is a staple in many households. It gives a Bloody Mary a distinctly savoury note and makes a versatile rub for meats of any kind, particularly lamb.

Most celery salts are made using only the seeds, however we like to incorporate the leaf foliage as well, which bulks up and balances out the mix.

20 g (¾ oz/1 cup) celery leaves
3 tablespoons celery seeds
65 g (2¼ oz/½ cup) sea salt

Finely chop the celery leaves and lay them on a piece of baking paper to dry out. This usually takes a minimum of 24 hours.

Once the celery leaves are dry, put the celery seeds in a pestle and mortar and grind to a smooth powder. Alternatively, use a spice grinder if you have one.

Add the salt and grind the mixture to your preferred consistency. Mix in the dried celery leaves and store in an airtight container at room temperature for up to 6 months.

Asparagus-frond omelette with garlic scapes

Serves 4

This is a simple, new-season comfort dish, announcing the arrival of spring and welcoming some young produce fresh out of the garden or the wild, if you're lucky enough.

Depending on the maturity and sex of your asparagus crowns, the spears will have different girths and, for this dish, we do discriminate between the size, preferring the thinner, wispier fronds. Bear in mind that spears can grow 30 cm (12 in) a day, so any thicker stems will turn wild and wispy in no time.

You'll also need some garlic scapes, which can be cut from your plants as they approach maturity. Garlic begins its die-back process – the prelude to harvest – in early spring, so try to cut some of the greener shoots and harvest from a number of plants. Garlic scapes are incredible to cook with as they are subtle in flavour and can therefore be used more liberally.

1 tablespoon olive oil
12 fresh garlic scapes, finely chopped
2 bunches asparagus fronds, cut into 10 cm (4 in) lengths if thin and 2–3 cm (¾–1¼ in) if thick
6 organic, free-range eggs
20 g (¾ oz) good-quality parmesan, finely grated
sea salt and freshly ground black pepper
1 teaspoon chilli oil (optional) and crusty bread, to serve

Heat the olive oil in a mid-sized omelette pan over medium heat. Add the garlic shoots and sauté for 2 minutes, then add the asparagus fronds and sauté for another 2 minutes. Be sure not to overcook the greens; they're better left a little al dente.

Whisk the eggs in a bowl and season with salt and pepper, then whisk in the parmesan.

Reduce the heat to low, pour in the eggs and cook for 5–7 minutes on one side before flipping the omelette over and cooking for a further 2–3 minutes on the other side.

Serve drizzled with chilli oil, if using, and lots of crusty bread on the side.

If you can't find garlic scapes for your omelette (left), replace them with 2 garlic cloves.

CELERY

Apium graveolens var dulce

Celery is one of the most popular salad vegetables, second only to
lettuce, and is entirely edible, from its sought-after stems
to its foliage and seeds – even down to its roots. It is a close relative
of parsley; so much so, that celery and parsley were known as the
same thing in Ancient Greece.

Until the seventeenth century, celery was almost exclusively regarded as a medicinal plant. Its first documented culinary use was as a leaf herb, specifically – a substitute for parsley or lovage – and it wasn't until the eighteenth century that celery was used for its stalk. The first iconic stalk variety, Pascal, was commercialised throughout North America and marketed by handing out free samples to train passengers travelling through Kalamazoo, Michigan. The rest is history.

Celery is one of the four most toxic vegetables – along with spinach, capsicum and sweet potato – due to its commercial growing practices. This is because ethylene gas is used to blanch the stems and remove the bitterness. It is advisable that, where possible, you source organically-grown celery or, even better, grow it yourself. If you've ever wondered why organic or home-grown celery is more bitter than the commercial produce, there is your answer.

In 1614, Giacomo Castelvetro wrote in his book *Fruit, Herbs & Vegetables of Italy* that 'celery has great digestive and generative powers and, for this reason, young wives often serve celery to their elderly or impotent husbands'. The bitterness that made celery a force de jour many centuries ago has now been bred out to make it more palatable when eaten raw.

Nutritional value

Before it became a popular salad crop, celery was used to treat a range of ailments, from impotency to hangovers. It assists stomach, liver, bladder and kidney function and can be used to treat constipation and as a diuretic to break up gallstones.

Origin

Believed to have originated in the Mediterranean, where it still grows wild in the wetter regions.

Favourite variety

Any variety grown organically in the garden.

Seasonality/In the garden

Prefers a mild growing season and so can often be found entering the garden in late autumn or early spring. The key to developing crisp stalks that aren't too bitter is water. Celery's wild ancestors can be found in the damper regions of Europe, which implies it needs plenty of water to thrive.

FENNEL

Foeniculum vulgare

There are two main types of fennel: wild and sweet (or Florence).
Wild fennel has small, flat seeds that are used as a spice and wispy
fronds that can be used as a herb. The bulbing sweet fennel
is more of a vegetable, with thick layers of flesh and hollow stalks.
Fennel fronds are a great substitute for dill and chervil, while
the bulbs are zingy with a strong anise flavour when eaten raw.
Once cooked, their flavour becomes much more subdued and
the flesh sweet and caramelised.

Although its fronds and bulbs are highly prized, fennel's flowers hold most of its treasure. They are pungent and more dynamic than other parts of the plant, constructed with the same intricacy as a snowflake. The price of fennel pollen is almost on a par with saffron because it is painstaking to collect. But it's worth it for its hints of liquorice and lemon with a unique soft sweetness.

To collect the pollen, gather as many flower heads as you can, being careful not to pick from roadsides, which will have almost certainly been sprayed, then shake them onto a sheet of baking paper. The pollen and some flower heads will fall onto the sheet. While you won't reap more than a ¼ teaspoon pollen from a couple of full flower heads, you'll be left with the star ingredient for a spice rub that works equally well on chicken, fish and pork.

For one reason or another, *finocchio* (fennel in Italian; I can hear my mum yelping as I type those letters) has become quite an offensive swear word in that language. We're not exactly sure why, but one theory is that men seem threatened by multi-layered vegetables that taste like Sambuca.

Nutritional value

Fennel is known as a warming herb, meaning it brings blood to the surface of the skin.

It also contains the flavonoid quercetin, an antioxidant that is anti-carcinogenic and, therefore, is used by cancer patients following chemotherapy. The most potent part of the plant is its seeds, which are high in anethole oil and used to treat indigestion and gas. Fennel tea, made by steeping dried and crushed fennel seeds in boiling water, has always been used in my family to reduce eye irritation and inflammation.

Origin

The coastal regions of the Mediterranean.

Favourite variety

Bronze fennel, which is a wild, non-bulbing variety with delicate bronze-coloured fronds and an intense anise flavour.

Seasonality/In the garden

Fennel enjoys both autumn and spring conditions, and can be found along roadsides in abundance from late spring to early summer when they begin to flower and produce their highly sought-after pollen. Bulbing varieties do best in cooler conditions, while wild fennel, used exclusively for its fronds, thrives at much warmer times of the year.

Other uses

Keeping a pot of fennel near your dog's kennel will help deter fleas. You can also make a natural flea spray using fennel.

Braised Florence fennel

(Compotée de fenouil)

Serves 4

4 fennel bulbs
1 tablespoon unsalted butter
1 tablespoon olive oil
1 onion, chopped
250 ml (8½ fl oz/1 cup) white wine
sea salt and freshly ground black pepper

To prepare the fennel bulbs, cut the tops and bottoms off and remove the two outer leaves, which are too tough to eat. Rinse the bulbs well and cut into 1 cm (½ in) thick slices.

Heat the butter and olive oil in a large saucepan over medium heat and fry the fennel and onion for about 5 minutes. Season with salt and pepper, then add the wine and cover the pan with a lid. Reduce the heat to low and braise for 20 minutes.

Fennel flower grappa

Makes 500 ml (17 fl oz/2 cups)

This is one very grown-up drink. It is one for the men and women of the old country and, if you grew up in Italy, this drink will definitely take you back to your childhood. Otherwise, it will make you behave like a child, so there are no losers here.

The grappa's intense aniseed flavour from the steeped fennel flowers makes it a seriously good mixer with ice, fresh lime and soda water or prosecco.

6–8 fennel flower umbels
500 ml (17 fl oz/2 cups) unflavoured grappa

Choose the freshest flowers for maximum flavour to make your grappa.

Wash and dry the flowers, then spread them out on a wire rack and leave to dry for 2 days in a cool, well-ventilated area.

Once dry, pack the dried flowers into a large sterilised glass jar or bottle (see page 14) with an airtight lid. Pour over grappa and leave to macerate for 8 days.

To finish, line a fine-mesh sieve with a piece of muslin (cheesecloth) and strain the grappa. Store in a sterilised glass jar or bottle in the refrigerator and drink cold.

Serve your grappa (left) straight from the fridge as a digestif with some bitter chocolate on the side.

LEEK

Allium ampeloprasum

The leek is a less sulphurous and much sweeter cousin of onion and garlic, making it the most accessible member of the allium family for younger children. Its subtle flavour combined with its hefty size makes it a home-grown staple. In a family of slow movers, leek is one of the slowest, requiring an extended growing period that sees it occupy the garden for up to a full year before it matures.

Its slow growth makes it tolerant of substandard care, particularly later in its life cycle. Mature plants will shoot densely packed flower heads that are oniony and sweet and a major culinary coup, so if space isn't a big consideration, leave some plants in-ground to blossom.

The roots of the leek are dense with flavour and minerals, and its nutrients more bioavailable in raw form than in mineral supplements. Because the roots tend to be quite tough and fibrous, they are best used in longer-simmered dishes or cooked in soups. Leeks are often grown in sticky, sandy loams, so make sure to soak them in water and rinse off any sand and grit before preparing.

A vegetable with as long a history as leek is bound to be linked to a few folklores. The great Roman emperor Nero was known as the 'leek eater', or 'porophagus', as he believed that eating the vegetable would aid his singing voice. Another legend is that British troops to King Cadwallader used leek hidden inside their helmets to help identify friends from foes. Finally, during the Middle Ages, women in Wales would sleep with a leek under their pillows on St David's Day so they could meet their future husbands in their dreams. It has since become their national symbol.

Nutritional value

Along with onions and garlic, leeks are an excellent source of vitamin K, vitamin C, magnesium and iron. They are thought to support energy movement and help tone the body, so whenever you are feeling emotionally or physically down, help yourselves to this vegetable. They also decrease blood-cholesterol levels, preventing the formation of blood clots and development of cardiovascular disorders.

Origin

Have been cultivated for over 3,000 years and originate from the eastern parts of the Mediterranean and into west Asia.

Favourite variety

Bulgarian Giant, which is a popular European variety with long, slender white stems.

Seasonality / In the garden

Like its cousins, the leek prefers to enter the garden in autumn when the soil is relatively warm. They then have a similarly long growing run – upwards of 6–9 months – until they are harvested at the turn of summer. Mature leeks will shoot flower heads, however the remaining stems will be in good condition, so an extended in-ground period is advisable if you can afford the space.

Soak the roots in fresh water for a couple of days, which will help clean the grit off and plump them up for cooking. Dust in besan (chickpea flour), deep-fry them and serve alongside steamed fish.

KOHLRABI

Brassica oleracea gongylodes

Sporting the suspicious appearance of an alien spacecraft, the kohlrabi is about as weird as vegetables get. It is, in fact, not a root vegetable, but a swollen stem, originally derived in the wild from a marrow cabbage. Thought to have originated in northern parts of Europe, it is still a staple ingredient in many countries, such as Germany and the Netherlands, where it is about as popular as the potato.

A member of the brassica family that includes cabbage, turnip and kale, it retains characteristics of each of those vegetables in its flavour, appearance and texture, but is as versatile as all three put together. It can be eaten raw, either shaved or sliced, steamed, stir-fried, baked, braised, stuffed or added to a hearty soup or stew. While cabbage can become sulphurous when cooked for long periods of time, kohlrabi is exempt from this sore point. The leafy stalks are great doused in tempura batter and deep-fried.

A vegetable that looks this funky has to be good for you and, along with a host of health benefits that include stabilising blood sugar imbalances, kohlrabi is also used in traditional Chinese medicine to stimulate the appetite and ease indigestion. The sliced and peeled stem of the kohlrabi, dipped in honey, can be used to help treat stomach ulcers.

Very small stems are primarily tough with fibrous skin, particularly on the base of the plant, so it's best to focus your harvesting efforts on the leaf foliage, which is a great substitute for kale. Letting plants go to seed will present you with optional yellow or white flower heads too, depending on the variety you're growing.

Nutritional value

Kohlrabi helps to improve energy, circulation and reduces stagnancy, which is a bonus for anyone feeling a little lazy. It's also an excellent source of vitamin C and potassium, is high in fibre and low in calories.

Origin

Coming from the German words *kohl*, meaning cabbage, and *rabi*, meaning turnip, it derives from northern regions of Europe.

Favourite variety

Azur Star, a slow-bolting, purple-skinned variety with crisp white flesh.

Seasonality/In the garden

Like all brassicas, kohlrabi is best suited to cool/mild conditions. Planting in autumn to early winter is recommended and, in cooler regions, they will grow well in early spring. They are hungry feeders that appreciate well-prepared and well-drained soil. If nutrition is inadequate or if they are left in-ground to overcook, flower production is inevitable.

The leaves of the plant are plentiful and can supplement the bulk ingredient of your favourite coleslaw. Make sure to leave enough foliage so as not to affect the elongated stem development.

PESTICIDES, FUNGICIDES & PLANT TONICS

Before we became tangled in synthetics, it was plants that had all the answers to our gardening dilemmas. And what do you know? They still do. Sometimes I like to think that for every problem that is presented, our planet possesses the solution in its natural resources. Perhaps that is a slightly romantic notion but, scientifically, we keep proving that most afflictions have a cure or treatment; it is just a matter of unravelling them.

What we put into our soils comes directly back to us in the foods we eat. On a very basic level, the more natural the process of growing food, the more natural – and we have to assume better – the food will be for us. There have been cases in our agricultural history where products once considered safe and used extensively in farming practices (Dichlorodiphenyltrichloroethane or DDT, for example) have been proven profoundly toxic and likely to be carcinogenic in nature. It is likely that we are still adopting less than perfect practices.

There is an obvious chain reaction that comes from using chemicals in the garden. Chemicals kill insects both good and bad, they sit in the soils for long periods of time and then farmers develop a dependency on further usage for their crops. They are then consumed in the foods we eat.

We may also need to start reconsidering the way we use the by-products and waste of the meat industries to fuel our food.

While some guidelines are stringent when it comes to organic classification of foods, none currently dictate that blood and bone manures must come from organic meat and animals. It doesn't matter how the stock was bred or what went into their systems; bone meal gets the organic tick of approval regardless. This doesn't seem right.

The next time you get agitated by a few tiny flies on your zucchinis, or possibly a hole in your tomato, try to consider the balance of nature. Rather than throwing toxins or inorganic animal waste products onto the garden, why not create plant-based treatments? It makes sense for plants to use plants to grow – rainforests have been operating on the cycle of growth and decay for millions of years, and so can our gardens.

Chrysanthemum

Best for: aphids, mites and some caterpillars.

You must know a plant to fully appreciate it, and the chrysanthemum has proven itself to those in the know to be more than just a pretty flower. Chrysanthemum produces a natural chemical called pyrethrin, which is the key ingredient in a common organic insecticide. Pyrethrum spray, made by steeping the dried petals in boiling water, can be used to control a number of sucking pests, from aphids to mites, and has also proven effective on a variety of caterpillars.

20 g (¾ oz/½ cup) dried
   chrysanthemum flower heads,
   coarsely ground
1 teaspoon pure soap flakes
1 teaspoon vegetable oil

Combine the chrysanthemum flowers with 1 litre (34 fl oz/4 cups) warm water in a bucket or jug. Cover and steep for 3 hours. Strain the liquid through a fine-mesh sieve into a spray bottle, discarding the flowers. Add the soap flakes and oil and shake vigorously, and it's ready to use.
   We recommend wearing a mask when spraying and to only spray in the early morning or evening when bees aren't active, as this spray is toxic to bees. The spray will remain effective for 12–24 hours, so only make up as much as you need.

Stinging nettle compost tea

Best for: plant tonic/natural fertiliser for fruiting plants, roses and annuals.

Stinging nettle first appears in early spring, just in time to make a nitrogen-rich plant tonic to feed your hungry warm-season crops. Making this tea is no different to making any brew, it's just on a slightly larger scale and uses a prickly plant. You'll need adequate hand protection, a large-sized bin and, preferably, rainwater to soak the foliage in. This compost tea will last more than 6 months and, along with nitrogen, will provide trace elements such as magnesium, copper, zinc and calcium.

1 bucket stinging nettles
rainwater

Wearing protective gloves, coarsely chop the stinging nettles inside the bucket (it will be easier to handle the tea later if the trimmings are short). Fill the bucket with rainwater, cover and leave in a sunny position for 2 weeks, stirring every 1–2 days. A foamy crust may form on the top and the tea will smell, so don't brew it inside. The brew will be ready after 2 weeks, but may need a little longer in cold weather.
   Strain the clear liquid through a piece of muslin (cheesecloth) or any old piece of fabric into a sealable container. Discard the stinging nettles and dilute one part tea in ten parts water to fertilise your plants. Apply the tea to the base of plants. It will last up to 6 months.

Green manure

Best for: nitrogen fixing.

A green manure refers to a crop of usually leguminous plants that is used to fix the soil with nitrogen. This process typically takes place during winter to provide a ground cover for plants and help promote microbial activity, suppressing weed growth and helping to bring nutrition in the soil closer to the surface. Incorporating a high level of organic matter into the veggie patch improves water infiltration and retention and aeration.
   You will need a mixture of seeds to sow in autumn or early winter, such as barley, wheat, feed oats or ryecorn. Also include plenty of beans and peas to replenish nitrogen as well as mustard seeds; their root system will control eelworm or nematode infestations.
   Scatter your seed mix generously over your veggie patch, lightly rake and water in well. The green manure crop will take about 2–3 months to mature to a dense, knee-height crop. At this point, use a garden fork to pull it up and break it down well, digging the soft green plants and roots back into the soil.
   It will break down and rot quickly and your garden beds will be ready for planting 2–3 weeks later. Plants will grow with wonderful vigour and have a really noticeable disease resistance.

Elder leaf spray

Best for: black leaf spot, powdery mildew, aphids and root pests.

The history of the elder tree is linked to witchcraft and potions. This leaf spray might not work to ward off evil spirits, but it will certainly take care of black spot and mildew. These fungal diseases stem from a lack of airflow through the garden and some plants, usually those with larger leaf foliage, are more susceptible than others. This spray is made using the leaves of the elder tree, which have antibacterial properties and help to sterilise the plant.

250 g (9 oz) elder leaves
1 tablespoon pure soap flakes

Bring 500 ml (17 fl oz/2 cups) water to the boil in a saucepan and add elder leaves, being sure to fully immerse them in the water. Boil for 30 minutes, then strain the leaves through a fine-mesh sieve and leave the liquid to cool until lukewarm. Dissolve the soap flakes in another 500 ml (17 fl oz/2 cups) fresh lukewarm water and combine the liquids. It is now ready to use as an antifungal spray.

Chive spray

Best for: powdery mildew, apple scab and black/brown spot.

Powdery mildew is a common fungal disease that likes to target large-leafed, warm-season crops, such as zucchini, pumpkin and cucumber. Unlike other fungal conditions, it doesn't need wet weather to thrive but, being a parasitic fungus, requires living plant tissue on which to grow. Frosts will usually kill the spores, so areas that don't get any typically struggle with it. Powdery mildew is lazy and does best when conditions are dry and when competition from other fungal spores is diminished. Chive spray throws a hefty challenge at it, and thanks to its antibacterial qualities, will quickly control the issue with regular use.

30 g (1 oz/1 cup) chive flowers, firmly packed
washing up liquid

Steep the flowers in 1 litre (34 fl oz/4 cups) boiling water in a bowl and leave to stand until cool. Once cooled, add a few drops of washing up liquid, which helps the solution to stick, and it is ready to spray on crops to help alleviate apple scab, powdery mildew and black/brown spot.
   Garlic chives can be used in the same way to fight against aphids and spider mites, in addition to fungal issues.

Horseradish spray

Best for: brown rot, aphids, whiteflies and insect repellent.

It makes sense that something as powerful as horseradish would have a practical garden application. The root contains isothiocyanate compounds, which are sulphuric and, when chopped, the chemicals become volatile from air exposure, giving it its distinguishable heat. When preparing horseradish for culinary use, vinegar is often added to control this process but, used in the garden, it can be used to treat brown rot and combat a number of sucking pests, such as aphids and whiteflies. Like people, plants will handle horseradish's heating properties differently, so it's best to spot spray and wait 24 hours to check for any adverse effects.

¼ horseradish root, roughly chopped
240 g (8½ oz/2 cups) hot chillies, roughly chopped

Bring 3 litres (101 fl oz/12 cups) water to the boil, then add the horseradish root and hot chillies. Remove from the heat and leave to steep for 1 hour, then strain the liquid through a fine-mesh sieve into a large container and allow to cool. Discard the solids. Decant into a spray bottle for immediate use.

Garlic fungicide

Best for: mildew, black leaf spot and insect repellent.

Garlic has long been regarded for its medicinal qualities. In fact, all members of the allium family are endowed with antibacterial properties, making them a popular ingredient in remedies to cure the common cold. This spray helps take those qualities into the garden. Heavily scented and packed with cleansing qualities, a garlic spray will cleanse a plant of a lot of its unwanted occupants, from powdery mildew and black spot, to sucking pests such as aphids, thrip and whiteflies. You should always have garlic spray at your disposal as it also comes in handy if you're suffering from unwanted love attention.

3 crushed garlic cloves
1 tablespoon chilli flakes
1 tablespoon vegetable oil
1 teaspoon washing up liquid
water

Mix the garlic cloves and crushed chillies in a large bowl or bucket, then add the vegetable oil, washing up liquid and 1.75 litres (60 fl oz/7 cups) water. Mix well and decant to a spray bottle for immediate use.

GREEN & LEAFY

Leafy greens are the most nutritionally dense sources of vitamins and minerals that we have. They also grow the most prolifically out of all vegetables and many varieties are readily available throughout the year. Greens can be perpetually harvested; the more you pick, the more the plant will regenerate. It is proof of how domesticated plants have become and, once we slack off or ignore the produce, things change quickly.

It is not surprising that we eat greens given their nutritional value, but what is surprising is how quickly we turn our backs on them once they start to degenerate. Once greens are ignored or warmer conditions stress them, they enter their bitter flowering stage and are usually turned up and removed from the garden. Not only does this diminish your overall return on investment, but it also cuts short the opportunity to enjoy the different flavours, colours and textures the plants provide. Take rocket and mustard, for example. The pungent and spicy flavour of both these greens becomes even more pronounced once they bolt to seed, but this presents an opportunity to use the greens differently and reap greater culinary rewards.

Mustard seeds, which are the last effort of the plant to procreate, are used to make one of the most popular condiments on earth: mustard sauce. Only a plant past its state of perfection can supply the raw produce that is required to make it.

Just like the foliage of your violas or leaves of your pumpkin are not typically seen as greens, the flowers and seeds of greens are not often seen as produce in their own right. However, a slight shift in your aperture reveals a far broader and more interesting culinary landscape.

BASIL

Ocimum basilicum

Basil is more than just the 'king of herbs', or *l'herb royale* as it is referred to by the French. In fact, its name descends from the Greek word *basileus*, meaning king, and this humble herb is as steeped in culinary history as it is in cultural significance.

In Hindu culture, holy basil – a perennial variety of the plant – is placed in the mouth of the dying to ensure safe passage to God, while in parts of Europe it is placed in the hands of the dead for similar reasons. Although in Ancient Greece basil once represented hatred and was even considered to be a symbol of Satan, in the Greek Orthodox Church it is now used to sprinkle holy water.

Whether garnishing a bowl of fresh pasta or a steaming pot of pho, we all agree that basil is best used fresh and should be added after a dish has been plated. Overcooking dissipates the herb's volatile oils and, therefore, its flavour. Drying basil mellows the flavour even further, so it is best used fresh.

Delicate and problematic when new to the garden, basil becomes one of the tougher and more enduring warm-season varieties. Stems are best used early in the season when the plant is still young; as they age they become tough, bitter and fibrous, but this is when flowers begin to emerge. These multi-towered flower heads tend to have a more subtle anise flavour than the sweeter leaves, and picking them will redirect growing energy back towards the foliage.

Basil and tomato are well-documented companions on the plate, and this is often given as the reason they grow so well in close proximity. Basil has claims as a good insect repellent too, and planting it near windows will help to repel flies and cockroaches. It will also help repel whitefly, aphids and hornworm – some well-documented nemeses of the tomato.

Nutritional value

Basil has one of the highest concentrations of vitamin K as well as manganese, and it is a very good source of copper and vitamin A too. Long regarded for its potent antioxidants and antiviral properties, basil is also anti-inflammatory and can be used to treat headaches and menstrual pain.

Origin

Thought to have its roots in India, basil has been cultivated for more than 5,000 years, making it one of the oldest and most important herbs.

Favourite variety

Spicy globe.

Seasonality / In the garden

Basil is a warm-season and warm-climate herb that acts as a perennial (Holy basil) in more subtropical zones. It is predominantly an annual that will begin to flower and die back once conditions cool down. It favours a sun-drenched part of the garden and should only be planted once spring has exorcised its cold, erratic nights and air temperatures are consistently above 20°C (68°F).

Rosemary wood-infused chicken skewers

Serves 6–8

Most of us have access to a woody growth of rosemary, whether that's in our own gardens or a bush growing by the neighbour's gate. Cutting back the growth will not only help the plant regenerate, but it will provide the equipment needed for this recipe – and save on the cost of a packet of bamboo skewers.

4 zucchini (courgettes), thinly sliced lengthways
60 g (2 oz/2 cups) fresh seasonal herbs such as basil, coriander, rosemary, sage, mint and thyme, finely chopped
1 fresh green chilli, destemmed
2 spring onions (scallions), trimmed
2 garlic cloves
zest and juice of 1 lemon
4 tablespoons olive oil
500 g (1 lb 2 oz) free-range chicken breasts, cut into bite-sized cubes
salt and pepper
6–8 fresh rosemary sprigs, lower leaves removed for skewering

Bring a saucepan of water to the boil and blanch the zucchini ribbons for about 30 seconds, or until softened. Drain and set aside.
   Combine the fresh herbs, chilli, spring onions, garlic, lemon zest and juice and the olive oil in the bowl of a food processor. Pulse the mixture until it forms a coarse paste.
   Put the chicken in a bowl and mix in the paste. Cover with plastic wrap and leave to marinate in the refrigerator for 1 hour.
   Fold and weave the zucchini ribbons onto the rosemary skewers, alternating with pieces of marinated chicken.
   Heat a barbecue chargrill or chargrill pan to high and grill the skewers for 5 minutes, turning regularly, until cooked through.

Herb flower pesto

Makes 250 g (9 oz/1 cup)

If you thought that making a traditional pesto was the quintessential act of the warm season, you may need to reconsider. Cutting off the flower heads for this recipe will help the plants refocus on more foliage production while there is still time. It's the prelude to the harder cut-back of winter.
   Bringing together all the floral notes of these perennial (and some annual) herbs is not as complicated as it may appear at first glance; rather it's a well-balanced herbaceous mix that will lighten up any plate of pasta or warm salad. It will also have you reminiscing about the greatness of summer.

50 g (1¾ oz/½ cup) walnuts
1 garlic clove
2 spring onions (scallions), trimmed
40 g (1½ oz/2 cups) herb flowers such as basil, thyme, sage, oregano, rosemary, parsley, dill and fennel
125 ml (4 fl oz/½ cup) avocado or olive oil
½ teaspoon sea salt
¼ teaspoon cayenne pepper

Roughly chop the walnuts and toast in a dry, hot frying pan over medium heat for 2–3 minutes, tossing constantly. Set aside to cool.
   Roughly chop the garlic and spring onions and add to a food processor with the remaining ingredients. Pulse the mixture to a coarse paste and serve immediately or store in an airtight container in the refrigerator for up to 1 week, or in the freezer for up to 4 months.

This flower pesto (left) makes the most out of the flowering jungle of herbs that greets you at the end of autumn.

ROCKET

Eruca sativa

There's something sexy about rocket that we can't put our finger on. Various classical authors have referred to the plant as an aphrodisiac and its ability to revive sexual desire. Because of its reputation, it was even banned from monastery gardens during the Middle Ages.

The biggest challenge when growing rocket is picking enough foliage to prevent the plant from going to seed. Early on, it is susceptible to developing thick-stemmed seed heads, however when the plant is young they are relatively tender, easy to pinch off and perfectly edible. As the plant ages, the seed heads become tougher-stemmed and more plentiful, resulting in the emergence of flowers.

Further down the track, the flowers will form into seed pods, which are also edible. Unless you are a farmer there will be an oversupply of seed from even one plant, so pick these seed pods young. Often referred to as gargeer in Indian and Persian cuisine, they are commonly used for their spicy flavour.

Young rocket leaves have a mild peppery, mustard flavour, however as the plant matures in the warmer months, the bitterness and spice of the foliage intensifies. At this time, it's best stirred through soups or added to stir-fries to mellow the flavour. Rocket can also be used as a spicy substitute for basil in a pesto or, even better, combined together.

Nutritional value

Rocket is an excellent source of vitamins A and K, as well as copper and iron. It is high in certain phytochemicals that have been found to counter the carcinogenic effects of oestrogen and may offer protection against some cancers.

Origin

Mediterranean region, where it has been considered an important wild herb since Roman times.

Favourite variety

Wild rocket

Seasonality/In the garden

An annual variety, rocket is easy to grow from seed in full sun to part shade during most times of the year. Rocket is a member of the brassica family that includes broccoli, cabbage and kale. Like its siblings, rocket is best suited to cooler growing conditions, however it will thrive year-round. In the warmer months, it offers more of its lesser-considered parts, namely the flowers and seed pods. Picking off early seed heads will keep the plant focused on foliage. As the weather warms up, let it go to flower to make the most of its delicate and spicy flower heads.

Once the plant has flowered, it then develops seeded pods that can be pickled and served with gamey meats, or they can be eaten as a crunchy and spicy snack on their own.

We've used vodka for this liqueur (right), but the citrus notes of coriander flowers lend themselves equally to gin.

Coriander flower liqueur

Makes approx. 375 ml (12½ fl oz/1½ cups)

This is a really exciting way to capture the flavour of summer in a drink! You can drink it neat, but we prefer to serve it over ice with a slice of lemon or lime and a dash of soda water.

40 g (1½ oz/2 cups) fresh coriander (cilantro) flowers
55 g (2 oz/¼ cup) caster (superfine) sugar
375 ml (12½ fl oz/1½ cups) vodka

Pick the coriander flowers in the morning when they are fresh and cool. Discard the stems.

Place the flowers in a sterilised 500 ml (17 fl oz/ 2 cup) glass jar (see page 14) with a lid. Add the sugar and vodka and seal tightly. Shake vigorously to dissolve the sugar, then store in a cool, dark place for 2 weeks.

After 2 weeks, strain the liquid through a fine-mesh sieve into a clean jug, then strain again through a sieve lined with paper towel to remove fine pollen and debris.

Store in a sterilised glass jar in the freezer.

Pickled green coriander seeds

Makes approx. 170 ml (5½ fl oz/⅔ cup)

Through the course of the coriander plant's life its flavours change and intensify. From the earthy, crisp roots to the fragrant foliage, coriander packs the biggest flavour punch towards the end of its life.

What's great about pickling the seeds is how it mellows the coriander flavour, yet remains citrusy and herbaceous. At Oakridge Estate in the Yarra Valley, just up the road from our farm, chef Matt Stone (considered one of Australia's leading sustainable chefs) introduced me to pickled coriander seeds served with his liquorice-flavoured sorbet with blueberries and mousse. The warmth of these flavours infused with the sharp citrus crunch of the pickled green coriander seeds was incredible.

Use these pickled seeds whenever a dish would benefit from a citrusy note. They're great in marinades, pastes for curries and salsa, and are perfect served with meat, fish and seafood.

Store the pickled seeds in the pantry and, once opened, store in the refrigerator where they will keep indefinitely.

170 ml (5½ fl oz/⅔ cup) white-wine vinegar
1 tablespoon salt
100 g (3½ oz/2 cups) freshly picked green coriander seeds

Use a saucepan large enough to hold two 500 ml (17 fl oz/2 cup) jars. Fill the saucepan with water and bring it to a simmer over medium heat.

Combine the vinegar and salt with 170 ml (5½ fl oz/⅔ cup) water in another saucepan and bring to a simmer, stirring until the salt has dissolved.

Divide the coriander seeds between two sterilised 500 ml (17 fl oz/2 cup) glass jars (see page 14), then pour the hot brine over the seeds.

Wipe the rims of the jars and seal tightly with lids, then lower both jars into the hot water bath. Boil for 10 minutes, then transfer the jars to a wire rack and leave to cool. Once cool, store in a dark, cool place and refrigerate after opening.

CORIANDER

Coriandrum sativum

Coriander is the queen – and the king – of the root-to-bloom
movement, as it is edible in every sense. Polarising and prolific,
every part of this plant can be used, from the foliage to the
pungent green seeds that signal its imminent decline.

Coriander was first named by the Ancient Greeks as *koris*, meaning bedbug, apparently because it shares a similar scent. It is one of the world's most widely-used herbs, especially in warmer regions such as India, Africa, the Middle East and Mexico.

No part of coriander needs to go to waste. Even if you're frustrated by lack of foliage success, a simple shift in perspective will broaden your culinary horizons. From palatable mild stems, to intense roots and seasonal flowers, this plant is a one-stop shop for ingredients. Its crowning glory, though, has to be its sweet green seeds which, when dried, become one of the world's most popular spices.

Coriander leaves are very delicate and have a particularly short shelf life once harvested. It is best to pick from the ground, leaving the roots intact, and store in a cup of fresh water in the refrigerator. Wrap the leaves in plastic for maximum freshness. Seeds are most pungent and flavourful when fresh and green, however dried seeds will store better for up to 1 year. As the flavour quickly diminishes once crushed, it's best to use whole seeds or grind just before using.

Nutritional value

High in vitamins A, C and K, as well as iron and dietary fibre. Supports the spleen, stomach and bladder, and can help regulate energy and support perspiration, meaning it can be helpful in flushing fever. As a diuretic, it has been used to treat urinary tract infections.

Origin

Coriander grows wild throughout Western Asia and Southern Europe, but it's not easy to define its origins. Early evidence of the plant's existence has been found in Israel c. 7,000 BC, the tomb of Tutankhamen and the Early Bronze Age in Macedonia.

Favourite variety

Eureka, which is a slow-to-bolt variety with sweet and pungent leaves.

Seasonality / In the garden

Best grown during the cooler months of a temperate climate and should be kept away from excessive, hot sunlight. We typically plant in late autumn and enjoy prolific foliage growth through winter and into early spring. Once the soil heats up and the plant is deprived of moisture, it is quick to bolt to seed, producing pungent flower heads and, later, its sought-after green seeds.

Potato and rocket seed pod sabzi

Serves 2 as a side dish

This is an Indian-inspired side dish known as a sabzi, or dry curry. It uses very few ingredients – potato often being one of the staples – and here we have added young rocket seed pods for a little spice and crunch. Make sure to pick the seed pods while they are still young and tender; the older pods will become woody and hard, meaning you'll need to cook them for longer to soften them, which in turn diminishes their flavour.

200 g (7 oz) rocket seed pods
2 tablespoons sunflower oil
1 large potato, sliced
1 teaspoon ground turmeric
1 tablespoon chilli oil
¼ teaspoon garam masala
salt and pepper
garlic roti and raita, to serve

Pinch the tough tips off the rocket seeds pods (much like you would with beans). Rinse the pods thoroughly.

Heat the sunflower oil in a frying pan over medium heat and sauté the potato for 4–5 minutes.

Add the turmeric and chilli oil and season with salt and pepper, then mix to coat the potatoes. Reduce the heat to low and sauté for another 5–10 minutes.

Add the rocket seed pods and cook for another 5–10 minutes over low heat until the seed pods have softened but still have a little bite. Stir in the garam masala.

Serve with some garlic roti and a bowl of raita.

Brassica 'bits and pieces' Szechuan stir-fry

Serves 2

At the end of each cool season, I am left contemplating the ghosts of autumn past. The brassica plants, with heads long decapitated, are left to go wild, shooting florets that attract early foraging spring bees. In years past, these bits and pieces would go directly on the compost heap, diced up to make them more consumable for our worm friends. These days, I like to use them as the ultimate last-minute 'something out of the garden' dinner.

large bunch of brassica leaves
large bunch of brassica florets, leaves kept whole
60 g (2 oz) brassica stem, inner part only
1 tablespoon canola oil
1 tablespoon rice vinegar
2 tablespoons soy sauce
80 g (2¾ oz/½ cup) vertically sliced white onion
1 tablespoon sesame oil
1 tablespoon minced garlic
1 tablespoon grated, peeled fresh ginger
2 teaspoons Szechuan pepper
30 g (1 oz/¼ cup) chopped roasted peanuts, to garnish
sliced spring onions (scallions) and fresh coriander (cilantro), to garnish

Harvest flowering plants from the garden and take the most tender bits of the inner stem (peeling away the tough and fibrous parts), leaves and florets, then chop the leaves and dice the stem.

Heat the canola oil in a wok over medium heat and add the rice vinegar, soy sauce and sliced white onion. Sauté for 2–3 minutes, then add the brassica pieces, sesame oil, garlic, ginger and pepper. Sauté until cooked to your liking.

Garnish with the roasted peanuts, spring onions and coriander.

Parsley root fries
Serves 2

What lies beneath our herb garden staple, the parsley plant, is a big, fleshy, white root that's similar to parsnip. While parsnip has a more delicate, sweet flavour, parsley root could be described as something between a carrot and celeriac with hints of parsley and turnip.

As you're pulling out your parsley plants after they go to seed, save the roots for this quick snack. Parsley root is a good source of fibre and vitamin C. If you don't have parsley root, you can substitute it with parsnip in this recipe.

200 g (7 oz) parsley roots, peeled and sliced into thin fingers
2 tablespoons garlic powder
60 ml (2 fl oz/¼ cup) olive oil
salt and pepper, to taste

Preheat the oven to 200°C (400°F).

Combine all the ingredients in a large bowl and toss until the fries are evenly coated. Spread the fries in an even layer on a baking tray lined with baking paper. Bake for 25 minutes until the fries begin to brown.

BRASSICAS

Brassica oleracea

Commonly known as the mustard family, brassicas make
up a large proportion of our vegetable quota. Cabbage, brussels
sprouts, horseradish, broccoli and kale are all members
of this unpretentious family.

In all their forms, brassicas are packed with the rockstar molecule sulforaphane; one of the most potent antioxidants around. Sulforaphane is responsible for the pungent odour we associate with many brassicas: think the gassy, farty smell of sulphur. This powerful antioxidant is a strong anti-inflammatory, a detoxifier and a brain enhancer, and it helps build mitochondria in our cells. Mitochondria produce energy, affect how we feel day to day and help maintain brain and body strength as we age.

Nutritional value

An excellent source of vitamins C and K. The high content of flavanoids and other phenolic compounds – which act as antioxidants – make brassicas especially protective against cancer and heart disease.

Origin

Native to Western Europe, the Mediterranean and temperate regions of Asia.

Favourite variety

Kailaan

Seasonality / In the garden

Brassicas are true winter veg' and perform poorly in hot weather. Most leafy varieties are easy to grow from seed and can be simply spread in garden beds as the weather cools. The gorgeous, delicate flowers of mustard, rocket and kailaan can be enjoyed towards the end of the season in late spring and are especially good in savoury dishes for their distinctly vegetal flavour.

Other facts

Boiling brassicas reduces their nutrient content by up to 50 per cent. The best ways to cook them are steaming, microwaving or stir-frying, as this will retain their vitamin C and the antioxidant sulforaphane.

Did you know that members of the brassica family include:

Bok choy (pak choy)
Brussels sprouts
Cabbage
Cauliflower
Horseradish
Kale
Kohlrabi
Radish
Rocket (arugula)
Turnip
Watercress

PARSLEY

Petroselinum crispum

Parsley is the most widely used herb on our planet and transcends many different cultures. Its name comes from the Greek meaning 'rock celery', most likely for its tendency to sprout in rocky, inhospitable places. It was often worn as a crown to banquets to help stimulate appetite and good humour, and to ward off intoxication.

———

Its early history revolves around death, which in part might be because of its close association with fool's parsley, which is deadly. Parsley was not given to nursing mothers because it was thought to cause epilepsy in babies, however, over the course of time it was discovered to be harmless and so began its cultivation as an important culinary herb and digestive aid.

———

Although parlsey is seen primarily as a garnish, it can be used for so much more. It stands up well to heat, makes a good base for dressings and marinades, and pairs well with seafood. Parsley is a key ingredient in bouquets garnis, tabbouleh and salsa verde as well as being a standalone vegetable itself.

Once the plant progresses to the point of flowering, the seed heads should not be consumed due to their high concentration of apiole. In the Middle Ages plants containing apiole were used to terminate pregnancies. They are safe to consume in small quantities, but should be avoided by pregnant women.

Nutritional value

Amazing source of vitamins A and K, and high in vitamin C, containing three times the amount as oranges. It also contains twice the amount of iron as spinach. Parsley is a strong antioxidant and is also known for its diuretic and blood-purifying properties. It is also a digestive aid, used to help soothe upset stomachs, and is well known for its ability to freshen your breath.

Origin

Central Mediterranean region.

Favourite variety

Flat-leaf (Italian).

Seasonality/In the garden

Being a biennial plant, it will seed and flower in its second year before dying. The stems are crunchy and palatable, irrespective of age, however the root becomes tough and fibrous as it grows older, so is best eaten young. When the plant is stemming and shooting its flower heads, pick from the outer parts of the plant, leaving the central stem to develop.

The youngest stems are crunchy without being fibrous and are best cooked in soups and stews. The cleaned roots can be used in the same dishes as part of a bouquet garni.

CHICORY

Chicorium endive

I was alerted to the medicinal benefits of chicory by a local Greek woman who happened to be ripping our plants out from the nursery garden beds. One by one, she yanked them free, long taproot intact, and stuffed them into her bag. Often, we'd have plants disappear from the nature strip of the property but not from the shop itself, and here we were in broad daylight watching the thief in the act. She didn't see me approaching and, as I startled her, she pulled out a doctor's certificate and began pointing at it and speaking loudly in Greek.

Perhaps I was impressed by her audacity, but I let her keep the chicory plants and began researching. Turns out that chicory, or endive as it is otherwise referred to, is highly sought after for its long taproots that have medicinal properties. It is used to relieve stress and anxiety, help with insomnia, and is an anti-inflammatory. The roots are dried and ground into a mocha-tasting coffee substitute. There were clearly too many attributes for the Greek lady to ignore.

Chicory is a member of the daisy family and can be found growing wild throughout Europe, Asia and North America. It has many varieties, from the Italian favourite Radicchio to the delicate and pale Witlof. It was a Belgian farmer in the nineteenth century that stumbled across this variety as he dried the plants' roots in his cellar. There, he noticed extremely pale white leaves or 'witloof' sprouting from the roots, and so, a new crop was born. Today, Witlof is grown in low-light environments to help retain its blanched colour and mild taste.

Chicory is often considered a winter salad vegetable that becomes overly bitter in the warmer months, but this bitterness can be mellowed by braising or grilling the leaves. The inner protected leaf foliage is more tender, crisp and less bitter than the outer.

Nutritional value

Chicory is an excellent source of potassium and vitamin K, and a good source of calcium. Most of its nutritional value comes from the leaf ribs and roots that contain inulin, which can be used by diabetics to regulate blood sugar levels. It can also assist in treating gout and rheumatism.

Origin

Native to Europe, where it is commonly found growing wild.

Favourite variety

Radicchio, a popular Italian variety that has deep red-veined leaves and an almost white, crunchy heart.

Seasonality / In the garden

A cooler-season leafy green, chicory, and its many varieties prefer to be grown in the autumn and early spring. Because the bitterness of the plant (highly valued in some regional Italian cuisines) is accentuated by the sun that will open the leaves and turn them green, it is commercially grown in low-light grow rooms to keep them blanched.

Lemon verbena oil

Makes 250 ml (8½ fl oz/1 cup)

This oil is great on seafood or tossed through vegetable dishes. Because of lemon verbena's aromatic citrus flavour, it is also perfect with Middle Eastern-inspired dishes, such as tagines and couscous.

handful of lemon verbena leaves
1 lemon
250 ml (8½ fl oz/1 cup) good-quality olive oil

Slice the leaves very thinly with a sharp knife.
Zest the lemon using a vegetable peeler, then finely slice the zest.

Combine the leaves and zest in a sterilised glass jar (see page 14) and cover with the olive oil. Set aside to macerate for a minimum of 2 hours before sealing tightly with a lid. Use within 2 days.

Chicory coffee

Makes a 1 litre (34 fl oz/4 cup) pot

To make chicory coffee, you need to harvest the long taproots of your chicory plants before cutting, drying and roasting them.

Chicory coffee originated in France and stems back to 1808 and Napoleon's Continental Blockade, which resulted in a regional coffee shortage. During a civil war, as coffee supplies dwindled, soldiers began to add roasted chicory root to their coffee grounds to make them go further. While the root doesn't contain any caffeine, it does have a malty, chocolatey flavour similar to mocha, making it the ultimate natural decaf.

5–6 mature chicory plants, long taproots removed

Cut the roots into ½ cm (¼ in) pieces and lay on baking trays to dry at room temperature until all t he moisture has been extracted.

Preheat the oven to 220°C (430°F).

Transfer the dried roots to baking trays lined with baking paper and roast in the oven for 1 hour, or until golden and crisp.

Transfer to a food processor and blend the roasted roots into a powder. Store in an airtight container at room temperature for up to 1 week, in the refrigerator for up to 6 months, or in the freezer for up to 1 year.

Chicory root is a popular coffee substitute (left) in Mediterranean countries such as Greece and Italy.

LEMON VERBENA

Aloysia citrodora

Also known as lemon bee brush for its ability to attract this important pollinator, lemon verbena is a pungent, lemon-scented flowering plant that grows wild in western South America. It was originally popularised by Europeans in the eighteenth century as a fragrant cosmetic oil, but has since become a popular cooking ingredient in both savoury and sweet dishes.

Early attempts to import the plant to mainland Europe saw it quarantined and left to rot with a host of other plant species. However, lemon verbena was one of the few to survive. This demonstrates its toughness and ability to cope with neglect; a buoy to hopeless gardeners everywhere. It has slim green leaves that are sandpaper-coarse and proficient in administering paper cuts.

Bruising the leaves releases their fragrant flavour, which is commonly used to infuse ice creams, sorbets, jams and yoghurts, but it is also popular in meat and fish dishes, and in salad dressings.

Lemon verbena leaves can be used as a substitute for lemon zest, but due to their coarseness they should be surgically sliced and have their stem lines removed. The plant produces dark red and white flower heads reminiscent of holy basil, and these can be added to dishes for decoration.

Along with green tea, lemon verbena tea can be used to assist with weight loss by suppressing hunger. It also has the additional benefit of reducing muscular damage while not prohibiting your stamina and ability to grow muscle. This makes it perfectly suited to any pre-workout routine.

Nutritional value

Its essential oils are high in antioxidants and can be used as supplements or infused as a tea to protect against muscle damage during exercise. Lemon verbena oil also helps relieve stress and anxiety and boosts the immune system.

Origin

Native to western parts of South America where it grows wild in the tough and inhospitable environment.

Favourite variety

Common lemon verbena.

Seasonality/In the garden

A perennial herb in warmer regions and one that dies off and goes woody in cooler areas (though it will reshoot once heat returns to the soil in spring). Its leaves have a high oil content and zesty lemon scent that are great for infusing foods, while its flowers – most prolific during summer and into autumn – are edible and decorative. It is a good idea to cut the plant back during winter to help promote new growth.

DILL

Anethum graveolens

Another member of the parsley family that also includes its closely-related cooking substitute fennel, dill is a top-to-bottom edible plant. Like coriander, it has the propensity to quickly bolt to seed, producing intricate flower heads loaded with pollen. At this time, the plant is at its most flavoursome and has the best medicinal benefits.

Dill gets its name from a Norse word, *dilla*, meaning 'to lull', as it was used to soothe agitated babies. The bible also refers to it being given to children during church sermons as a means of keeping them quiet.

Once a wild weed, it is a commonly used herb in the northern European regions of Scandinavia and Russia, where it is paired with cold-water fish, particularly salmon and herring. More broadly, it is used to flavour dill cucumbers, utilising the strongly-scented seeds to infuse the pickling juice. If you want a delicious snack that also improves your gut health, look no further than dill pickles.

Dill leaves are so delicate and don't tolerate prolonged heat during cooking so, much like basil, they are usually added near the end of the process or used as a garnish. The dried herb is weaker in flavour so needs to be added more liberally. Dill is chlorophyll-rich and antibacterial, and chewing dried seeds after a meal can help to freshen your breath.

Nutritional value

Most of the nutritional pungency of dill comes from its seeds, which are high in vitamins A and C and low in saturated fats and cholesterol. Dill also aids indigestion and helps to relieve insomnia, menstrual cramps and stomach pain.

Origin

East-Mediterranean Europe and parts of West Asia.

Favourite variety

Mammoth, which is a tall-growing variety very good for pickling.

Seasonality / In the garden

Dill is a little temperamental in the garden, preferring the mild air temperatures and warm soil that come with autumn and early spring. In the winter months, frost can severely damage the delicate leaf foliage. Similarly, it becomes stressed by hot summer conditions, where it grows tall and leggy, shooting seed heads and producing flowers.

Did you know?

Adding a few sprigs of dill to cabbage when cooking will nullify its unpleasant smell.

Fennel and dill seed breath freshener

Makes approx. 625 ml (21 fl oz/2½ cups)

Along with the memory of a great dish, another thing
that is prone to linger is stale breath, and bad breath,
like body odour, can be difficult to self-diagnose.

Therefore, it is best to take precautions by keeping
a healthy supply of this breath freshener on hand.
In India, this seed mixture, known as *mukhwas* (*mukh*
meaning mouth and *vas* meaning fresh), is available
to chew on throughout the day, particularly after
meals. Not only does it remove stagnant saliva
to help freshen your palate, it also aids digestion.

40 g (1½ oz/1 cup) fennel seeds
1 tablespoon lime juice
1 teaspoon salt
170 g (6 oz/1 cup) sesame seeds
40 g (1½ oz/½ cup) dill seeds
2½ tablespoons linseeds (flax seeds)

Combine the fennel seeds in a bowl with the lime
juice, salt and 2 tablespoons water. Stir, then set
aside for 10 minutes to allow the seeds to absorb
the moisture.

Heat a dry frying pan over medium heat and toast
the fennel seeds for 5–10 minutes until lightly brown,
stirring regularly to stop them burning. Transfer the
seeds to a plate to cool.

Repeat with the other seeds, toasting them
separately as they will all brown at different speeds.
Transfer them to a plate to cool.

Once all the seeds are cool, mix them together
and store in an airtight container for 6–12 months.
Take a pinch of the seeds and chew for an instant
breath freshener.

Fried anchovies in herby breadcrumbs

Serves 4 as an entrée

This is a great little side dish that you can serve as an entrée or with a summer-time grazing lunch. The herb sauce really makes this dish; it is punchy and full of fresh, herbaceous flavours. The strong fishy and salty flavour of the anchovies is balanced out by the zest of the herbs.

If you're looking to freshen your anchovy breath after overindulging on this dish (who'd want to, but maybe you've got a hot date) try munching on the breadcrumbs without the garlic.

500 ml (17 fl oz/2 cups) olive oil, for deep-frying
12 anchovy fillets in oil, drained
35 g (1¼ oz/¼ cup) plain (all-purpose) flour
2 organic, free-range eggs, lightly beaten

Herby breadcrumbs
1½ tablespoons fresh dill foliage and stems
1½ tablespoons fresh flat-leaf (Italian) parsley foliage
  and stems
handful of garlic scapes (if these are not in season
  use ½ garlic clove)
zest of ½ lemon
150 g (5½ oz) fine breadcrumbs from day-old white
  bread (crusts removed)
sea salt and freshly ground black pepper

Herb and chilli sauce
2 tablespoons fresh dill foliage (and flowers if
  in season)
2 tablespoons fresh flat-leaf (Italian) parsley foliage
1½ tablespoons fresh oregano foliage (and flowers
  if in season)
½ garlic clove
1 red chilli
juice and zest of ½ lemon
60 ml (2 fl oz/¼ cup) extra-virgin olive oil

To make the herby breadcrumbs, finely chop the dill, parsley and garlic, then mix together in a bowl. Season with salt and pepper and set aside.

For the chilli and herb sauce, finely chop the dill, parsley and oregano and crush the garlic. Remove the seeds from the chilli and finely chop the flesh. Combine all the ingredients in a bowl and set aside.

Heat the oil in a large, heavy-based saucepan until it reads 180°C (350°F) on a cooking thermometer, or a pinch of breadcrumbs dropped into the hot oil browns in 20 seconds.

Dip the anchovy fillets first in the flour, then the egg and dredge them in the herby breadcrumbs, pressing down gently to coat. Repeat the crumbing process again, then deep-fry the anchovies, in two batches, for about 2 minutes until golden. Transfer to a wire rack with paper towel underneath to catch excess oil.

Serve warm, drizzled with the herb and chilli sauce.

LOVAGE

Levisticum officinale

Lovage, or Love Parsley, is also known as love-ache; *ache* being
a medieval word for parsley. It shares characteristics with both parsley
and celery, but is stronger in flavour. The plant's stalks and stems
were once blanched like celery, but as celery grew in popularity
as a salad vegetable, lovage was left behind.

Though lovage has fallen out of favour in the kitchen, all parts of the plant can be used. The leaves can be chopped up and added to any dish that calls for celery or parsley, including salads, soups and stews. The stems that hollow out as the plant ages are a good substitute for single-use plastic straws, adding a unique flavour to your Bloody Mary. Its seeds can be used as a spice and, in some parts of Eastern Europe, the root is peeled and used as a vegetable.

Lovage has gained a strong foothold in gardening and for its medicinal uses. As a companion plant, lovage helps to repel flying insects like whitefly, aphids and thrip. The seed heads are made up of hundreds of tiny flowers that provide nectar for adult mosquito-sized parasitic wasps, which then lay their eggs in soft-bodied garden pests, such as caterpillars. When the eggs hatch, they destroy the pest by eating it from the inside out.

Medicinally, lovage excels due to its antiseptic properties that help to flush out urinary infections while providing relief from inflammatory complaints; in particular, arthritis. It also increases perspiration and strengthens your immune system.

Nutritional value

High in vitamins C and K and rich in calcium, lovage is a great source of antioxidants, helping to relieve indigestion and heartburn.

Origin

Native to southern Europe and also grows wild in parts of Asia.

Favourite variety

Sea lovage, a perennial with reddish-green stems and glossy leaves that help increase blood flow to the brain.

Seasonality/In the garden

Lovage is a leafy perennial plant that stales off during the winter, but is capable of surviving very cold seasons. It is one of the first plants to respond to the emerging spring, and the best time to plant is early spring or mid-autumn. It will tolerate a semi-shaded space and is great for attracting beneficial insects, such as ladybirds, to your garden.

Chermoula

Makes 250 ml (8½ fl oz/1 cup)

Traditionally used as a marinade or relish in North African cooking, chermoula can be used to flavour seafood, fish, meat and vegetables. It is especially good with fish and lamb.

1 red onion
4 garlic cloves
1 bunch fresh coriander (cilantro) leaves, stems and roots
1 bunch fresh lovage leaves and stems
2 teaspoons coriander seeds
1 teaspoon whole black peppercorns
1 teaspoon chilli flakes
2 teaspoons cumin seeds
1 teaspoon sea salt
1 teaspoon ground turmeric
1½ teaspoons ras el hanout
185 ml (6 fl oz/¾ cup) olive oil
juice of 1 lemon

Roughly chop the onion, garlic, coriander and lovage, including the stems.
   In a dry frying pan over medium heat, toast the coriander seeds, peppercorns, chilli flakes and cumin seeds for 1 minute, until lightly toasted and fragrant.
   Combine all the ingredients except the oil and lemon juice in a food processor, and process for 1 minute. With the food processor on low speed, slowly drizzle in the olive oil until a thick paste forms. Stir in the lemon juice.
   Either use immediately to marinate your meat or refrigerate in an airtight container until required. The chermoula will keep for 2–3 days in the fridge.

Avocado and egg on toast with mustard flowers

Serves 1

All the classic breakfast ingredients are here: eggs, toast and avocado. Give them a morning kick-start by adding a garnish of fresh mustard flowers. You can also use rocket or other brassica flowers in their absence, but we prefer mustard for its spice.

1 organic, free-range egg
½ ripe avocado
1 teaspoon extra-virgin olive oil
1–2 teaspoons freshly squeezed lemon juice, to taste
1 slice bread
white-wine vinegar
1 tablespoon mustard flowers
salt and pepper, to taste

Place the egg in a small saucepan, cover with cold water and bring to the boil over medium–high heat. Boil for 5 minutes, then remove from the heat and run under cold water to stop the cooking process. We like our eggs semi hard-boiled but, if you prefer your eggs fully cooked, leave them to boil for another 2–3 minutes. Once cool, peel, then cut the egg into ½ cm (¼ in) thick slices.

In a bowl, mash the avocado with a fork and mix in the olive oil and lemon juice. Season to taste with salt and pepper.

Toast the bread and spread the mashed avocado on top. Arrange the egg slices on the avocado and finish with a light drizzle of vinegar, a sprinkle of salt and pepper and the mustard flowers. Serve immediately while the flowers are still fresh and punchy.

MUSTARD

Sinapis alba

Pungent and hot, mustard greens are a cool-season crop
that increase in spice and bolt to seed as the weather heats up.
There are many varieties of mustard, including mizuna and
bok choy, however these are typically not considered part of the
mustard family. Traditional mustard varieties include Indian
(which has darker seeds), Chinese (lighter seeds)
and leaf mustard, which is grown for greens.

Most commercially available mustard greens tend to be light in colour with crinkled or ruffled leaves (similar to kale), however our favoured varieties are the darker-leaved ones such as Giant Red, Osaka Purple and French Brown. Generally, as the weather heats up, the spice and pungency of the leaves increases to match. A little goes a long way.

The seeds of the plant are used to create the iconic condiment, mustard, which is made by mixing the ground seeds with vinegar, oil and seasoning. As a general rule, the darker the seed the spicier the mustard. Although there are now French, English and American varieties, it has been a popular condiment since Ancient Egyptian times.

When using raw mustard greens, select the younger inner foliage that will be crunchier, tender and less spicy than the outer. The broader, outer leaves are best sautéed and make a great accompaniment to steak or fish. The leaves and stems can also be pickled, along with the flower heads, which add extra colour.

Nutritional value

Excellent source of vitamin K and a very good source of vitamins A and C, and calcium. Helps with blood circulation and is anti-inflammatory, so could assist with cold symptoms, sprains and arthritis.

Origin

Comes from the Himalayan region of India and has been consumed for more than 5,000 years.

Favourite variety

Giant Red, for its broad, burgundy-coloured leaves that shoot yellow flower heads once conditions warm up.

Seasonality / In the garden

Like all brassicas, mustard greens do best when the weather is cool and prefer an autumn entrance into the garden. Early spring is also a great time to plant, but as soon as the plant experiences heat stress it will shoot flower heads. When young, the flower heads can be cut back to help refocus growing energy on the foliage and are the perfect stems to sauté along with a nice cut of beef. Once the flower stems harden, the foliage becomes overbearingly spicy. At this point it's best to let them go to seed and make your own condiment.

WEEDS & FORAGING

Dig into the history of vegetables and you'll find that all descended from plants found in the wild. Over time, these plants were eaten and the best were saved and perpetuated. The most palatable varieties became the domesticated vegetables we eat today. As we have been trained to go looking along supermarket shelves for our food, we have forgotten that many of the foods we eat today can still be found in the wild, most prolifically even in our inner-city gardens.

Foraging your own food is an important part of the root-to-bloom movement because it makes the most of nature's bounty. How often do you find yourself battling to grow seasonal crops only to find that 'weeds' keep thriving on your neglect? Rather than fighting the forces, we simply have to give in to the will of nature. If the conditions best suit dandelions, chickweed or wild mustard (all perfectly edible), we should develop our eating habits to match and focus on what will be plentiful.

Many restaurants now like to build a menu around seasonal food that can largely be foraged. Not only because it's resourceful and environmentally conscious, but because it's the best representation of the seasons and their flavours. Just like the vegetables we grow in our gardens, food found in the wild has its seasons too. Wild brassicas and chickweed are typical of winter, just like dandelions are most prolific in spring and purslane summer.

Of course, foraging food does come with a particular set of risks. Who knows if the roadside grass where the wild fennel grows was recently sprayed by the council?

There's also every chance that the modern-day pristine pastureland or bushland was once the site of a big, ugly factory. Even the more remote parts of our country aren't exempt from poor practices. In fact, I was a little taken aback recently by a man riding a quad bike, wearing a full body suit and face mask, spraying along a quaint country road. So, if in doubt, it's always best to play it safe and pick from areas you know are untouched.

If you took a walk through your garden – right this minute, in fact – you would probably be surprised at what food lies unnoticed amongst your lawn, in the cracks of your pavement or disguised between the crops in your vegetable garden. Foraging in your own garden, where you are certain that no harmful chemicals or pesticides have been used, always throws up more than you can imagine. Perhaps it's not the most satisfying of adventures – you probably envisioned a remote coastal destination rather than the driveway of your suburban property – but it is certainly the most accessible and food-mile conscious way of collecting food.

LEMON MYRTLE

Backhousia citriodora

A native, fragrant evergreen tree that grows prolifically in Australia's subtropical coastal regions, but is now grown in other parts of the word, including South Africa and the southern parts of the United States and Europe. The lemon myrtle – also known as the lemon verbena tree – was once known as lemon-scented myrtle until the name was shortened to better promote and brand it in culinary circles. It is now one of Australia's most popular and recognisable bush foods and has been used by Indigenous Australians as both a food and a medicine for centuries.

Considered the queen of the lemon herbs, lemon myrtle has a strong aroma of citrus with delicate menthol essence and a strong lemon flavour, which is both sweet and refreshing. The essential oil extracted primarily from the leaves, but also the flowers and fruit, can be found in many personal care and beauty products such as body lotions, lip balms, soaps and shampoos.

One of the most common culinary applications of the plant is the use of leaves to make a great antioxidant herbal tea, which is served either hot (to soothe) or cold (to refresh). More extensively, lemon myrtle is used for its citrus flavour in both sweet and savoury dishes, such as marinades, soups, casseroles and roasts. Because the flavour is so intense, like bay leaves, only one or two leaves are required to infuse a dish.

Nutritional value

High in calcium, zinc and magnesium and has good amounts of vitamins A and E. It has the most concentrated source of plant citral, which contains powerful antimicrobial and anti-fungal properties used to treat warts, cold sores and acne. It is also a powerful source of antioxidants, typically ingested as a tea.

Origin

Central and south-eastern Australia.

Favourite variety

Common lemon myrtle.

Seasonality / In the garden

The lemon myrtle tree can grow to over 20 m (65 ft), but is typically bushier and stands at approximately 5 m (16 ft). It thrives in Australia's subtropical coastal regions, but also grows well in more temperate climates further south where it produces highly fragrant flowers, fruit and leaves. The plant flowers in the summer and is typically followed by fruit, and both fruit and flowers are great attractors of native birds and beneficial insects for the veggie patch. Being an evergreen plant, foliage is always available.

Lemon myrtle and lilliput caper mayonnaise

Makes 500 ml (17 fl oz/2 cups)

This is a great twist on your classic mayonnaise. It is divine served alongside a platter of chilled lobster or prawns (or any seafood really). It is also a great sauce served with a summer spread of grilled fish or vegetables.

3 organic, free-range egg yolks
60 ml (2 fl oz/¼ cup) lemon juice
1 teaspoon white-wine vinegar
125 ml (4 fl oz/½ cup) peanut oil
125 ml (4 fl oz/½ cup) olive oil
¼ teaspoon ground lemon myrtle
50 g (1¾ oz/¼ cup) lilliput capers, rinsed and drained
7 g (¼ oz/¼ cup) chopped flat-leaf (Italian) parsley
sea salt and freshly ground black pepper

Combine the egg yolks, a pinch of sea salt, some pepper, lemon juice and vinegar in a food processor. Blend on medium–high speed while slowly drizzling in the oils. When the mayonnaise is thick and creamy, transfer it to a clean bowl and fold in the lemon myrtle, capers and parsley. Check the seasoning, adding more salt, pepper and lemon juice if needed.

Pickled wild fennel flowers

Makes 500 ml (17 fl oz/2 cups)

Pickling these wild blooms adds a whole new depth to their light aniseed flavour and sharp tang. They also make a wonderful substitute for capers. Harvest wild fennel flowers from late spring well into the hot summer, but be sure not to pick wild fennel from urban locations or roadsides that may have been sprayed with chemicals.

50 g (¾ oz/1½ cups) wild fennel flowers
500 ml (17 fl oz/2 cups) white-wine vinegar

Wash and dry the flowers, then leave them to dry completely on a wire rack in a well-ventilated, cool place. This should take about 2 days.

Place the flowers in a 750 ml–1 litre (25½–34 fl oz/3–4 cup) sterilised glass jar (see page 14) and add the vinegar. Press the flowers down until they are fully submerged in the vinegar. Seal the jar tightly and leave to macerate for 5–6 weeks in a cool, dark place. The pickled flowers will last up to 1 month after opening. Store in the refrigerator.

Wild rocket risotto

Serves 6

Wild rocket has a sharpness and heat to it that you just don't get from freshly planted rocket seedlings. The wonderful creaminess of risotto mellows out the rocket's bite. Serve with lots of parmesan and a crisp green side salad.

100 g (3½ oz) wild rocket
1 litre (34 fl oz/4 cups) vegetable stock
1 tablespoon extra-virgin olive oil
2 red onions
½ celery head, finely chopped (including the leaves)
2 garlic cloves
350 g (12½ oz) arborio rice
100 ml (3½ fl oz) dry white wine or dry vermouth
2 tablespoons butter
100 g (3½ oz/1 cup) freshly grated parmesan cheese
sea salt and freshly ground black pepper

Wash the rocket well. Bring a large saucepan of salted water to the boil. Blanch for 2 minutes, then remove with a wire skimmer or slotted spoon and drain well. Roughly chop the leaves and set aside.

Heat the stock in a large saucepan. Heat the olive oil in a large frying pan over medium heat and sweat the onion and celery with a pinch of salt for 3–4 minutes. Add the garlic and cook for another 2 minutes. Increase the heat to high and add the rice, stirring continuously for 2–3 minutes. When the rice looks translucent, add the white wine and continue to stir.

Once the rice has fully absorbed the wine, reduce the heat to a simmer and begin adding the stock, one ladleful at a time. Be sure to let the liquid fully absorb between additions. Cook for 15 minutes, adding the stock and stirring regularly. Test the rice to see if it's cooked – it should be al dente – then season with salt and pepper to taste.

Remove from the heat and stir in the butter, parmesan cheese and wild rocket. Serve immediately.

If you can't get hold of wild rocket for this recipe (left), salad rocket works just as well.

WILD BRASSICA

Wild brassica oleracea

A member of the brassica family and a biennial, though
sometimes perennial plant, the leaves of the wild brassica don't
form a tightly packed head like the cultivated variety. Instead,
they are wild and wispy, typically producing sparse foliage quickly
followed by long-stemmed flower heads. There are more than
a dozen varieties of wild brassica in Australia, including mustard
greens, broccoli, cabbage and turnip. Much like the domesticated
plants, the wild flowers and youngest leaves can be added to
salads, while the older foliage is best cooked or wilted.

There are a few identifying features of wild brassica. The most obvious one is thin, long stems that shoot flower heads from the centre of the plant. When flowering, the leaves appear alternately spaced on the emerging stem and each flowering part will have exactly six stamens (the male reproductive part) and, of course, its most distinguishable yellow (sometimes white) flowers. Each flower has four petals in the shape of a cross and it is from these flowers that the family gets its name: Cruciferae, meaning 'cross-bearing'.

Walking through any wild landscape or park, at any time of year, it is impossible to avoid wild brassicas. Although, the best time to forage for them is during the cooler months of winter and early spring when the leaves are more tender and less bitey. As conditions warm up and the moisture dries out, the plants' pungency can become overwhelming.

Nutritional value

Wild brassicas share the same genetic make-up as their domesticated cousins, making this family one of the most nutritious and beneficial to your health. Very high in vitamin C and minerals such as potassium and iron, they are also endowed with antioxidants, which make them part of the anti-cancer family of vegetables.

Origin

Southern and western Europe.

Favourite variety

Wild mustard, which has spicy leaves punctuated by peppery yellow flower heads.

Seasonality/In the garden

Wild brassicas are typically biennial plants that flower twice before dying off, but some are perennial. They can be found at any time of year and in most places, though they are most prevalent in early spring when they are more easily distinguished by their long-stemmed flower heads. Leaves are most tender and palatable early in the cool season, becoming spicier with age and heat.

RED CLOVER

Trifolium pratense

Most of us would be more familiar with hunting the elusive four-leafed clover as a symbol of good luck than foraging the plant for food. Red clover, however, is another unlikely edible plant, with the leaves having a faint bean-like flavour. The blossoms, which are similar in appearance to onion flowers with tightly-packed bunches of electric purple to crimson red flowers, can also be eaten fresh or dried and infused to make a sweet-tasting herbal tea. It is also the national flower of Denmark.

In traditional Chinese medicine, red clover is believed to clean the blood, reduce heat and remove toxins. It is used as an alternative medicine for reducing the hot flashes that occur during menopause and diminishing the effects of PMS. Historically, red clover blossoms have been used in herbal medicine to treat respiratory problems, skin inflammations (such as eczema), liver disease and cancer as well as joint problems. The native Indians of North America used it topically to treat skin wounds.

Though generally considered safe to consume, some people may develop a headache or rash after consuming red clover. It may also interact with certain medications, including blood thinners, birth control pills and other drugs that affect hormones, so it is best to trial moderately at first and always consult with a doctor. It is advisable not to eat red clover if you are pregnant or breastfeeding.

Nutritional value

One of the richest sources of isoflavones, which are water-soluble chemicals that act like oestrogen and can therefore be helpful in reducing hot flashes and the effects of PMS. Red clover is also thought to help lower cholesterol, improve urine production and improve circulation. It is relatively high in calcium and magnesium, as well as vitamins B and C.

Origin

Eurasia

Favourite variety

Common red clover.

Seasonality / In the garden

A member of the legume family, red clover can be used to add nitrogen to the soil when grown as a Green manure (page 62). It typically thrives during the cooler months either side of winter and flowers most prolifically during summer, however is a perennial herb that grows year-round. It is a hardy plant and will grow with relative ease, surviving with moderate water and sunlight.

High in protein, you can dry the flowers and leaves and store them in a jar to be used when they are out of season.

OXALIS

Oxalidaceae

The name is derived from the Greek word *oxus* or *oxys*, meaning 'sour'. This is due to the plant's sour, acidic taste, though it could also be described as zesty and citrus-like. All members of this family – of which there are over 500 varieties – are high in oxalic acid, which makes the leaves refreshing and zesty to chew, but can also be slightly toxic. When eaten in large quantities, it can interfere with kidney function and proper digestion.

———

Oxalis weed, which is most commonly referred to as wood sorrel, is often confused with clover as its leaves are superficially very similar. It is distinguishable, however, by its tart flavour that makes it a great last-minute addition to omelettes, stews and fresh salads. Both oxalis and clover are low ground covers with similar flowers that have three leaves attached to short stems. But, while clover has oval-shaped leaves, oxalis leaves are heart-shaped with a crease through the centre that allows the foliage to fold in at night or in heavy rain.

———

All above-ground parts of the plants are edible, from the leaves, which are usually green but sometimes appear reddish depending on the variety and season, to the stems and flower heads.

Nutritional value

As its name suggests, oxalis is very high in oxalic acid, which gives it its zesty taste, but can be toxic if consumed in large amounts. It is high in vitamin C and has good levels of vitamin A. As a medicinal plant, it is believed to help reduce fever and increase appetite. Applied topically, it can reduce skin inflammation.

Origin

South America.

Favourite variety

Yellow sorrel, which is often mistaken for clover and known as 'sour grass' due to its flavour.

Seasonality/In the garden

Most varieties of oxalis germinate and flourish in early spring and bloom in summer. They are perennial plants that die back in the winter – dying off completely in very cold zones – but bounce back once the warmer weather arrives. They cope well in shaded areas of the garden and, due to their tough and durable root zones, are able to out-manoeuvre more favoured crops.

Best used in moderation mixed through salads. Can also be fermented and eaten pickled.

DANDELION

Taraxacum officinale

Dandelion's name comes from a Latin word meaning 'tooth of a lion', and was given to describe the plant's jagged long leaves. Its French nickname, *piss-en-lit*, refers to its diuretic qualities and literally translates to 'wet the bed'. Though it is one of the more commonly known edible weeds, it is still largely under-utilised both in food and in medicine. The plant appears in early spring, becoming more prevalent and noticeable thanks to the pop of its yellow flowers and the formation of its seed heads that resemble fluff balls. Every kid has whispered many a wish into their cupped hands over a dandelion seed head.

The composition of the seed heads allows the plant to spread far and wide, where they shoot long and deep taproots that make them difficult to pull from the ground. It's these roots that are used for making a coffee substitute (see page 86); similar tasting, though not as rich in colour as chicory coffee. Dried leaves can be brewed to make a tea and the flowers can be used to make dandelion wine.

The young leaves of the plant lend a hint of bitterness to a green salad and are most palatable and mild in early spring. As the warm season progresses the more bitter the foliage becomes, making it more suitable for wilting or using in soups and stews.

A favoured dish is using the young crowns of the plant, which can be found bursting through the soil in late winter. Cut them free from the taproot, just below the surface of the ground and sauté in olive oil and garlic; so simple and so (bitter) sweet.

It is possible to grow blanched dandelion leaves through winter in much the same way as Witlof. To do so, take a few long taproots from the ground in late autumn and bury them in pot of soil in a cool, dark place. Keep them hydrated and you should soon notice sprouting tender, pale-coloured leaves with the distinct scent of dandelion.

Nutritional value

The dandelion has always been prized for its medicinal use. It is used as a mild laxative, a diuretic and to aid digestion, and is very high in vitamins A and C, and high in iron and calcium. The root of the plant, which, like chicory, is dried and ground into a coffee-like substitute, contains inulin which lowers blood sugar levels in diabetics.

Origin

Eurasia

Favourite variety

Common dandelion.

Seasonality / In the garden

As with most plants in the garden, spring and summer – when there is the right mix of warmth and moisture – prove the best growing conditions for dandelions. Mid-spring is when you will begin to notice them popping up all over the place, with the flowers following soon afterwards.

Batter-fried sow thistle

Serves 6

4 organic, free-range eggs (3 left whole and
  1 separated)
300 g (10½ oz/2 cups) plain (all-purpose) flour,
  plus extra for dusting
1½ teaspoons finely ground sea salt
200 ml (7 fl oz) ice-cold sparkling mineral water
30 g (1 oz) coarse sea salt
1 kg (2 lb 3 oz) sow thistles
500 ml (17 fl oz/2 cups) extra-virgin olive oil

To make the batter whisk the whole eggs in a bowl
until light and fluffy, then add the flour, egg yolk
and finely ground sea salt. Whisk until well combined.
Slowly add the ice-cold water, whisking constantly.
(It is important to add the water very slowly or the
batter will become too thin.) Refrigerate for 2–3 hours
to let it rest, then whisk the remaining egg white to
soft peaks and fold into the batter right before you
use it.

To de-thorn the thistles, it's recommended you wear
a pair of gloves. Discard the roots and any foliage then
peel the remaining stems to remove the thorns and
wash well. Cut the stems into 5 cm (2 in) long pieces.
Bring a saucepan of water to the boil, add the coarse
sea salt and boil the thistle stem pieces for 15 minutes.
Drain, pat dry with paper towel and set aside.

Heat the oil in a large frying pan over medium
heat until it reaches 180°C (350°F) on a cooking
thermometer. Dip the thistle stems into the
batter then straight into the hot oil. After about
90 seconds, turn the stems over, then remove
when lightly golden. In order to maintain the
oil temperature, only fry 10 stems at a time. Once
cooked, transfer to a wire rack with paper towels
underneath to catch excess oil. Serve immediately
while still warm.

Dandelion flower syrup

Makes 500 ml (17 fl oz/2 cups)

Make the most of these weeds popping up all over
your lawn and harvest the dandelion's gorgeous
flowers. This syrup is a quick and easy recipe to make
and will add a very sophisticated flavour to desserts
and drinks.

35 g (1¼ oz/1 cup) dandelion flowers
350 g (12½ oz/1 cup) honey
juice of 1 lemon

Wash the flowers and dry well in a salad spinner.
Combine the flowers in a saucepan with 250 ml
(8½ fl oz/1 cup) water, ensuring all the petals are
submerged. Bring to the boil over high heat and cook
for 5 minutes, then reduce the heat to medium–low
and simmer for a further 25 minutes.

Depending on your preference, you can leave the
flowers in the syrup or strain them out using a fine-
mesh sieve. Add the honey and stir until dissolved,
then add the lemon juice and mix well. Leave to
cool, then transfer to a sterilised glass jar or bottle
(see page 14) and store in the refrigerator for up to
1 month. The honey will act as a preservative so
your syrup lasts longer.

Dandelions deteriorate quickly once picked, so be ready to make this syrup (left) straight away.

SOW THISTLE

Sonchus oleraceus

Out of all the edible weeds, sow thistle, or milk thistle as it is commonly referred to, seems the least likely to be eaten. Closely related to the dandelion – both members of the sunflower family – it has tall stems with clusters of small yellow flowers and glossy, easily bruised leaves that emit a milky sap when broken. Sap from any plant is usually an immediate turn-off, however sap from sow thistle has medicinal properties that have been utilised by Indigenous Australians for generations.

The Latin name for sow thistle alludes to its edible nature, with *oleraceus* meaning 'leaf vegetable'. While it is often seen as just another weed with a prolific ability to self-seed far and wide, it is also a highly nutritious leafy green. The young leaves of the plant, which are less sappy than the older leaves, can be used as a substitute for lettuce and silverbeet. In southern parts of Italy, it is considered a good eating plant that is often sautéed and served with pasta.

In your own garden, it can be viewed as either a friend or a foe. Older plants are particularly susceptible to aphids, which can spread disease to other plants, though it helps lure other beneficial insects such as hoverflies. As a hungry nitrogen feeder, it will compete with your more prized crops, so it is best to remove once you stumble across them; unless sow thistle is your vegetable of choice.

Nutritional value

Sow thistle is a good source of vitamins A and C, as well as calcium and iron. The sappy juice from the plant is used as a herbal medicine to cure ulcers, and it also has value as a laxative, which can help cleanse your system and flush out kidney stones. Some ancient literatures attest that chewing on it will purify bad breath.

Origin

Europe, Asia and North Africa.

Favourite variety

Common sow thistle.

Seasonality / In the garden

Sow thistle is an annual plant related to the dandelion that grows mostly during the cooler times of the year, before flowering in spring to summer (in Australia's coolest regions) and dying off. You'll find young plants all around the southern parts of Australia in late winter. In spring it flowers with yellow blossoms, followed by fluffy seed balls, both very similar in appearance to the dandelion.

PURSLANE

Portulaca oleracea

This is a small, succulent-like plant that you are just as likely to find in the cracks of your concrete driveway as in a park or bushland. Its seeds have been ground and used to make dampers and breads by Indigenous Australians and the indigenous people of South America, to which purslane is native.

Rather than being viewed as a weed, it is seen in many parts of the world as a crop in its own right, as well as a beneficial plant that assists other crops. Its roots grow deeply and with ease through even the toughest of soils, which enables the roots of less vigorous plants such as corn to follow the path towards deeper soil, allowing them access to more nutrients and moisture.

Eaten raw it has a slightly sour and salty taste, albeit with a mucus texture due to its succulent-like nature, but is still very palatable and great in mixed salads. It can also be wilted or deep-fried, tempura style, or pickled and preserved. While nasturtium seeds are used to create Poor man's capers (page 146), purslane seeds are used for the female version, Poor woman's capers.

A study in Maryland, USA, found that egg yolks from chickens that were fed purslane contained a staggering 10 times more omega-3 fatty acids than those fed on normal feed. Given how well omega-3 fatty acids help to reduce cholesterol, there is a strong case for keeping your own chooks and feeding them on this commonly found 'weed'.

Nutritional value

Purslane has the highest amount of omega-3 fatty acids of any vegetable, and is very rich in antioxidants and vitamins A, B and C.

It is thought to help with constipation, urinary infections and haemorrhoids. It has also been used externally to treat insect bites and eczema.

Origin

South America.

Favourite variety

Common purslane.

Seasonality/In the garden

Purslane loves heat and, thanks to its succulent-like composition, will thrive in dry conditions. You will notice it popping up around late spring and, by mid-summer, it will have overrun areas where it is allowed to sprawl. Although it is largely seen as a competitive weed, it can in fact help the rest of the veggie patch by providing cover for the soil; a pseudo mulch of sorts. It can also break through tougher zones, allowing other plants' roots to access deeper supplies. Flowers come in late summer followed by the seeds, which form as clusters of pods, each containing hundreds of tiny, hard black seeds.

Pick the youngest foliage tips and make a simple salad dressed in olive oil and lemon juice with salt and pepper to taste. This is a fresh and nutritious side dish to baked fish.

SAMPHIRE

Salicornia europaea

Samphire is a smooth-skinned, succulent-looking coastal plant. It is found among the rocky outcrops and mudflats of Australia's southern coastal zones and is known by a number of names, including glasswort, pickleweed, sea bean and perhaps the most apt, sea asparagus. If you love wild-foraged asparagus, this is a saltier, crunchier variety that is easier to come by provided you know where to look.

This tough plant has a woody base that shoots clusters of long, succulent tips; from afar it looks like a field of rubber grass. Growing in tidal zones means the plant is built to survive harsh conditions and has a thin outer layer protecting its stems, or leaves, from the wind, sun and salt.

In a culinary sense, samphire has come full circle in recent years. In Britain, it used to be given out by fishmongers as a free seasonal special with cod fillets and, as Hugh Fearnley-Whittingstall observed, was typically left to rot in the bottom of the fridge. However, more recently, it has become a popular foraged vegetable, served at some of the best restaurants.

There is a lot to admire about samphire. It tastes vaguely like fennel; it even has similar umbrella-shaped flower heads (that are edible too), though it can sometimes be more bitter, particularly the older, reddish tips. Its saltiness and crunch, which is best in the younger, green tops of the plant, is reminiscent of well-salted asparagus. Finely chopped raw, it is ideal for seasoning salads or sautéed and mixed with butter, lemon and a dash of olive oil as a side dish to fish.

Nutritional value

Very high in vitamin A and high in vitamins B and C, samphire is loaded with essential minerals, including magnesium, calcium and potassium. It has almost no fat content and the foliage contains compounds called fucoidans – often found in sea vegetables – which are known to have anti-inflammatory and antioxidant effects.

Origin

Coastal regions of northern Europe.

Favourite variety

Common samphire.

Seasonality / In the garden

Samphire can be found in coastal, saltwater zones, such as tidal rivers and mudflats, at all times of the year. Its young and delicate green foliage is most prevalent during the warmer months because it turns a pinkish, red colour and loses some of its fresh crunch in winter. At all times of the year, there are some of these salty, asparagus-like stems to be found. Later in summer it shoots flower heads that are edible and commonly pickled and, after this, its seed, which is known to be used in bread-making.

CHICKWEED

Stellaria media

Chickweed is a highly nutritious, plentiful cool-season annual that you'll find occupying idle and empty soil space during winter. Its botanical name derives from Latin, with *stellina* meaning 'stellar' or 'star', referencing the shape of its tiny white flowers. *Media* means 'between' or 'intermediate', referencing this plant's preference to nestle in empty space rather than grow over the top of something.

————

While most edible 'weeds' are usually strong and bitter, chickweed is quite the opposite. It is as sweet and delicate as fresh pea shoots, and highly nutritious too. It is best eaten raw in salads or sandwiches as a substitute for sweet greens. Given that it is found during the cool season, it is also a great ingredient for soups and stews.

————

Chickweed is ideal for getting a jump-start on attracting and feeding pollinators and other beneficial insects early in the season, as it is one of the first flowering plants with prolific blooms. Organic farmers have been using it for generations as a soil indicator, as it usually grows only where the soil is high in nitrogen and phosphorus and retains adequate moisture. If the plant is found stunted, your soil lacks nitrogen; if it's pale, phosphorous; if it's absent from where it once flourished, moisture.

Nutritional value

Chickweed is high in iron, calcium and potassium, and very high in vitamin C. It also has good levels of vitamins A, B and D. It has been said to aid weight loss as it curbs appetite and acts as a diuretic, helping those who eat it to lose fluid. It can also soothe mucus membranes and help to ease respiratory conditions such as asthma and bronchitis. In folk medicine, it has been used to treat itchy skin by steeping the stems in hot water and applying externally to affected areas.

Origin

Europe

Favourite variety

Common chickweed.

Seasonality/In the garden

Chickweed is a cool-season creeping annual that forms a mat of oval-shaped leaves with tiny white flowers. It is not as bullish as other species that are considered 'weeds' as it has a very shallow root structure and can be easily removed. It does, however, have thick-set flower heads that contain tens of thousands of seeds that are easily dispersed. Rather than coming across chickweed in a thickly matted lawn area, you'll find it growing in more open, idle parts of your garden. We often find chickweed occupying empty pots during the winter time, which, by spring, are completely engulfed. As soon as the heat hits, it shoots to seed and begins to brown off and die.

Samphire salad

Serves 4

This is an incredibly simple way to enjoy samphire, served as a side dish with grilled fish or seafood. Its fennel-like flavour also makes it a great accompaniment to pork and gamey meats. Be sure to use only the tender, green tips of the samphire sprigs for this salad.

300 g (10½ oz) samphire

Dressing
juice of 2 lemons
sea salt and white pepper
extra-virgin olive oil, to taste

Wash and drain the samphire.

Make the dressing by combining the lemon juice, salt, pepper and oil in a jar. Seal and shake vigorously to combine.

To serve, simply arrange the samphire on a platter and dress with the salad dressing.

Chickweed soup

Serves 4

Homely and hearty, this is a winter soup with a nutritious kick.

4 tablespoons unsalted butter
2–3 garlic scapes, chopped
2 small potatoes, peeled and diced
750 ml (25½ fl oz/3 cups) chicken or vegetable stock
2–3 large bunches of young chickweed leaves
250 ml (8½ fl oz/1 cup) thick (double/heavy) cream
sea salt and freshly ground black pepper, to taste

Heat the butter in a large saucepan until melted and foamy, then add the garlic scapes and sauté until soft. Add the potatoes and enough stock to cover them, then cook over medium–high heat until the potatoes are tender when pierced with a sharp knife.

Add the chickweed and continue cooking for 5–7 minutes, then remove from the heat. Leave to cool, then transfer to a blender or food processor and blitz to purée. Once processed, return to a clean saucepan, add the remaining stock and bring to the boil. Take off the heat and stir in the cream. Season to taste with salt and pepper.

QUEEN ANNE'S LACE & HEMLOCK

When driving through the country in the summer, you're likely to see an abundance of Queen Anne's Lace and its poisonous cousins growing wild along the roadside and in the surrounding fields. When we first moved to the Yarra Valley, I noticed clusters of these white flowers growing everywhere. Consultation with our local botanist confirmed that this now-naturalised plant, Queen Anne's Lace (*Daucus carota*), is a wild carrot flower and is completely edible. This advice also came with a warning: don't mistake it for hemlock, which will kill you.

We let it go wild in the greenhouse as a foraged edible flower. The flower head is composed of an umbel of tiny white flowers with one small, deep red flower at its centre, and the story goes that the red flower symbolised a drop of Queen Anne's blood, where she pricked her finger making lace. It's this tiny red flower in the middle of the umbel that differentiates it from its poisonous cousin hemlock (*Conium maculatum*) and a number of other poisonous relations, which are often mistaken for Queen Anne's Lace.

Hemlock (*Conium maculatum*) – also known as poison parsley, devil's parsley, devil's porridge, beaver poison and fool's cicely – is a member of the carrot family, but it is one of the most poisonous plants in history. All parts of the plant contain the alkaloid coniine, which causes stomach pains and vomiting followed by progressive paralysis and death.

In the famous oil painting *The Death of Socrates* by French artist Jacques-Louis David (1787), Socrates is sentenced to death and is executed by drinking a cup of poison hemlock.

Fool's parsley (*Aethusa cynapium*) is another confusing herb in this family, and is closely related to hemlock. Though it is almost indistinguishable from hemlock, it is not quite as poisonous. A post-mortem examination

from death by consuming fool's parsley shows redness of the lining membrane of the gullet and windpipe, and slight congestion of the stomach. Since some toxins are destroyed by drying, hay containing the plant is not poisonous.

False Queen Anne's Lace (*Ammi majus*) – not edible but commonly used for flower arranging – contains large amounts of chemicals that can cause phytophodermatitis and hyperpigmentation. For humans, the main hazard is the compound furanocoumarin, found in the sap, which can cause skin burns.

True Queen Anne's Lace is a fantastic culinary herb. It has a beautiful scent of golden syrup and a fresh, sweet-carrot flavour. Mixed with sugar, the intensity of the sweet carrot undertones is enhanced. Its tiny white flowers are great in desserts, and the carrot flavour works well with liquorice and tart citrus. Like a garden carrot, the fronds of Queen Anne's Lace are edible and, if you pull up the plant, you'll find a lovely white carrot-like root that can also be eaten.

Although wild in nature, Queen Anne's Lace couldn't be more elegant in appearance.

FRUIT & FLOWERS

It should come as no surprise that flowers have always had a place in the human diet. It makes perfect sense that something as fragrant and colourful as a flower would be attractive to eat, even more than some vegetables like the humble potato, which needs to be dug up, boiled and, preferably, mixed with butter and salt to make it palatable.

Our senses of smell and taste are so closely aligned, and our palates are tempted by what we see, so it's unsurprising that flowers work so well in food. The familiar and heady scent of a rose petal or the fresh, sweet-pea crunch of a broad bean flower not only add another dimension of flavour to a dish, but are visually stunning too.

When I tell people I grow edible flowers for a living, their first question is always 'what makes your flowers edible?' The answer is nothing. My flowers are no more edible than the ones you grow in your garden. The only difference – in keeping with the root-to-bloom movement – is that I harvest the plant at different stages of its life cycle, utilising the flowers as opposed to yielding its leafy green foliage or ripened fruit. Most plants flower at some stage in their life cycle in order to form a seed for procreation and most of these flowers are edible.

The sensory and juicy fruit that we savour is, in fact, the ripened ovary of a flowering plant; the precursor to many different fruits, including orange, zucchini, pumpkin, almond and elderflower. Excluding tomatoes and other members of the nightshade family (capsicum, eggplant and potato, for example), whose flowers are poisonous to eat, most of the fruits that we enjoy every day begin as beautiful edible flowers.

Along with flowers and their fruits, leaf foliage – which is prolific and easy to find – is often edible too. Take the diverse family of the cucurbits, which includes pumpkin, zucchini and cucumber. All of their foliage can be used as a nutritious substitute for spinach. Perhaps the best part of cooking with foliage is that picking the leaves will not affect the ultimate prize of fruit, provided it is done in moderation.

ELDERFLOWER

Sambucus nigra

From its fleeting summer season of dainty and fragrant white flowers, to the sinister-looking black berries it yields in autumn, the elder tree summons a romantic and magical image in our heads. Elderflower has always been considered magical; a symbol of witchcraft and of sacrifice. Witches are said to be able to turn themselves into elder trees, and the leaves and berries were once used to break spells of evil intent.

It is believed that growing an elder tree in your garden will protect you from misfortune. In Europe, elder trees were traditionally planted in cemeteries to ward off evil spirits. Even Jesus is said to have been crucified on a cross made from elder wood as it is a tree of regeneration.

Today, the flowers and berries of the elder tree make luxurious ingredients for syrups and dessert flavourings.

Nutritional value

Elderflower is rich in bioflavonoids, commonly known for their antioxidant, anti-cancer, anti-inflammatory and antibacterial properties, and its flavonols offer valuable antiviral benefits. Chlorogenic acids, also present in elderflower, may assist with allergies, in the regulation of blood glucose levels and act as laxatives.

Origin

North America (American Elder), Italy and Switzerland (European Elder).

Favourite variety

Black Beauty (cultivar name: Gerda), for gorgeous plum-coloured foliage and pink flowers.

Seasonality / In the garden

Elder trees grow to 5 m (16 ft) tall. They have a preference for moist soils and are commonly found growing in damp, sheltered areas, but they also cope well with drier conditions. They have extensive root zones that are prone to suckering – that is, shooting up in different parts of your garden – so they will need to be contained to prevent them bullying out other plants.

Historical uses

Elder wood was often used to make butcher's skewers, shoemaker's pegs, needles for weaving nets and musical instruments. In the Scottish Highlands, the bark and roots were commonly used to produce a black dye, and the leaves to produce a green dye. The Romans also made a purple colouring from elderberries, which was used as a hair dye.

Did you know?

The leaves, bark and roots of most elders, including the American Elder, contain poisonous alkaloids and should not be consumed.

Elderberries are toxic when uncooked, so they should never be eaten raw. Although black elderberries are partially edible in their raw state, they may still cause nausea.

What else you can do with it?

A research study in Ireland demonstrated that elderflower extract is effective in killing several common hospital pathogens, such as methicillin-resistant Staphylococcus aureus (MRSA), or what we commonly call Staph infection. This research provided scientific proof of elderflower's antibacterial properties against most gram-negative and gram-positive bacteria, aligning its effectiveness with that of traditional medicines.

Elderflower marshmallows
Makes approx. 25

In the pecking order of childhood sweets, the marshmallow sits right at the top. No kid will refuse one of these soft and doughy treats, including this slightly more sophisticated take on the recipe. They may even attract some adult interest too.

neutral-flavoured oil, for greasing
½ tablespoon icing (confectioners') sugar, sifted
½ tablespoon cornflour (cornstarch), sifted
11 g (¼ oz) gelatine leaf
230 g (8 oz/1 cup) caster (superfine) sugar
½ tablespoon liquid glucose
1 organic, free-range egg white
1½ tablespoons Elderberry cordial (see opposite)

Grease a 13 x 15 cm (5 x 6 in) brownie tin with oil.
Sift enough icing sugar and cornflour to cover the base of the tin into a small bowl. Sprinkle over the base of the tin.
Put the gelatine leaf in a small bowl, cover with cold water, and leave to soak for 5 minutes.
Combine the sugar and liquid glucose with 100 ml (3½ fl oz) water in a saucepan and simmer over low heat until the sugar has completely dissolved. Increase the heat to high and bring the syrup to a boil. It is ready when a dollop of syrup dropped into cold water forms a pliable, hard ball (about 124°C/255°F). When the syrup is ready, plunge the saucepan into a sink of ice-cold water to stop the cooking process.
Squeeze the gelatine leaf to remove any excess water, then stir into the sugar syrup. In the bowl of a stand mixer, whisk the egg white to stiff peaks then, with the whisk still running, gradually drizzle in the syrup. Continue whisking until the mixture is thick and glossy, then add the elderberry cordial and whisk once more to combine. Pour the mixture into the prepared tin, smooth the top, and leave to set overnight at room temperature.
Sift the remaining icing sugar and cornflour onto a piece of baking paper, reserving a little for the top of the marshmallow. Turn the marshmallow slab out of the tin onto the baking paper and dust the top with the reserved icing sugar and cornflour. Leave to sit for 1 hour.
Using a sharp knife, cut the marshmallow into cubes and toss through the icing sugar to coat.

Elderflower syrup
Makes 500 ml (17 fl oz/2 cups)

Before realising how perfumed elderflowers could be, I would often simply stare at these plants, wondering about their purpose. The large clusters of tiny white flowers were completely odourless.
However, one fateful day, as a chef was harvesting the clusters of flowers from the garden, I was told they needed to be infused in sugar in order to draw out the scent. And so, my love affair with elderflower began.
Elderflowers are best gathered just as the tiny buds are beginning to open and some are still closed. Gather them on a warm, dry day as this is when their perfume will be at its most fresh and fragrant. Do not harvest elderflowers when they are wet.

6–8 elderflower umbels
115 g (4 oz/½ cup) caster (superfine) sugar

Place the elderflowers in a bowl and pour over 500 ml (17 fl oz/2 cups) boiling water. Cover and leave to infuse for up to 24 hours (the longer you leave it, the more intense the flavour will be).
Combine the elderflower water and sugar in a saucepan and simmer over medium heat for 3–5 minutes. Remove from the heat and leave to cool slightly, then strain the syrup through a fine-mesh sieve into a sterilised glass jar or bottle (see page 14). Store in the refrigerator for up to 1 month.
This syrup is delicious served over hotcakes and crêpes, or drizzled over a dessert.

Elderberry cordial

Makes 500 ml (17 fl oz/2 cups)

When we've spent the summer enjoying and yielding
from the elderflower tree, it's exciting to know that
those flower heads we left on the tree will turn into
luscious black elderberries come autumn. Now's the
time to make a cordial from the berries so it can
be enjoyed throughout the year.

This cordial is great mixed with still or sparkling
water or, even better, when used as a base for a
cocktail. And while you're sipping your libation,
it probably won't even dawn on you that elderberries
are incredibly nutritious. Often referred to as the poor
man's medicine chest, elderberries contain loads
of vitamin C. In fact, except for blackcurrants and
rose hips, they contain more vitamin C than
any other plant. Clinical research has even shown
that elderberry extract is an effective treatment
for flu, including swine and avian flu.

500 g (1 lb 2 oz) caster (superfine) sugar
500 g (1 lb 2 oz) elderberries (approx.)

Combine the sugar with 500 ml (17 fl oz/2 cups)
water in a large saucepan and bring to the boil
over medium–high heat. Stir until the sugar has
dissolved then add the berries and boil for about
20 minutes until the berries turn a brown-purple
colour. Continue stirring as the berries cook to make
sure the liquid doesn't catch.

Line a fine-mesh sieve with a piece of muslin
(cheesecloth) and strain the mixture into a clean
saucepan, squeezing the berries in the muslin
to extract all their juice. Return the cordial to the
heat and boil for a further 10 minutes.

Use a funnel to pour the hot cordial into sterilised
glass bottles (see page 14) with either swing-top lids,
sterilised screw-tops or corks. The cordial should be
stored in a cool, dark place and will be shelf-stable
for up to 1 year. Refrigerate once opened.

To serve, add a splash of undiluted cordial to fruit
salads, dilute one part cordial in four parts water for
fragrant ice blocks, or use it to add a sophisticated
spin to cocktails and mocktails.

VIOLA

Viola cornuta

Violas are ridiculous little romantics. Historically referred to by their more tender name, Love-in-idleness, they make numerous cameos in Shakespeare's plays, from *Hamlet* and *A Midsummer Night's Dream*, to *The Taming of the Shrew*. In Roman mythology, Cupid's arrow accidentally struck this little flower, turning the flower's juice into an erotic love potion.

We shouldn't disregard viola simply as potted colour in our gardens. This easy-to-grow annual plant is not only ornamental, but its leaves and flowers are edible too. Its beautiful and delicate flowers are coveted by the world's best chefs and adorn top restaurant dishes worldwide.

Not to be mistaken with the heavily-scented violet (*Viola oderata*), *Viola cornuta* has a neutral scent and a very slight lemony flavour. It is available in many different colours, from white and yellow through to deep red and black. Unlike *Viola oderata*, which has a short flowering period during the winter months, *Viola cornuta* will flower for most of the year in cool to temperate climates.

Nutritional value

Viola contains both vitamin C, for strengthening your immunity, and potassium, which supports heart and muscle function. The vivid colours of viola also suggests the presence of flavonoids, antioxidants and phytonutrients. These are all proven to protect your cells from damage and assist in lowering your risk of chronic diseases, such as cardiovascular disease and cancer.

Origin

A common European wildflower.

Favourite variety

Johnny Jump Up (or Heartsease), for its small lion-faced flowers and prolific self-seeding nature.

Seasonality / In the garden

Viola prefers the cooler weather but will tolerate heat as long as it finds some shade. It will flower from late winter through to early summer and can easily be grown from seed or seedling. If growing from seed, make sure to propagate a month or more before the last frost and then transplant into the garden mid-spring. Viola is relatively unfussy in its soil demands and will happily self-seed year after year.

Did you know?

The leaves can be used as a natural pH test to indicate acidity.

What else you can do with it?

Viola has long been used in herbal medicine for epilepsy, eczema and respiratory diseases, such as asthma, bronchitis, the common cold and chesty coughs. Yellow, green and blue-green dyes can also be made from the flowers.

ROSE GERANIUM

Pelargonium graveolens

The indestructible rose geranium can usually be found
overtaking a corner of your elderly neighbour's unkempt garden.
It's the sort of bush that goes unnoticed but really deserves
a little more credit and attention.

The abundant foliage yields large furry leaves that are high in oil and can be used for any manner of infusions to add a potent citrus flavour to your drinks and dishes. Its sweet lemon scent and striking, electric purple petals make rose geraniums one of my favourite edible flowers.

Pelargonium graveolens and *Pelargonium rosat* are popular scents in the perfume industry. I remember a participant at one of our edible gardening workshops exclaiming 'this plant smells like the Aesop store!' Right you were, sir. The foliage is distilled for its scent and the essential oil of rose geranium is commonly added to lotions and creams, not only for its rose scent but also its anti-inflammatory properties and ability to alleviate stress and mild pain.

Nutritional value

Rose geranium offers many nutritional and healing properties. A tea made with the leaves releases endorphins that aid in treating pain, and its organic compounds and chemicals will positively impact the endocrine system, relieving stress and anxiety-causing hormones.

A natural anti-inflammatory, rose geranium can be used topically to treat sore joints and muscles, and it has been shown to eliminate harmful gut bacteria. It also has antifungal properties, which boost immunity and help keep harmful pathogens in your body at bay.

Origin

Native to South Africa, Zimbabwe and Mozambique.

Seasonality/In the garden

Rose geraniums produce abundant leaf foliage throughout the year but only flower sporadically from spring to early autumn, yielding very few flowers. Growing in most soil types, they are very unfussy and require little care. To tame their unruly limbs, you can prune them back hard in the winter. They can also be easily grown from cuttings; just cut off the branches, remove the bottom leaves, plant in the ground and water regularly while they establish.

Flavour profiles

Although all geraniums are edible, the common geranium is rather tasteless, so choose scented geraniums like the rose geranium for its incredible flavour and scent. The leaves of scented geraniums are very high in aromatic oils and flavours and come in many different varieties, from rose and lemon, to chocolate, mint and orange.

Did you know?

Rose geranium is an effective natural insect repellent. Use a few drops of the essential oil on your skin and rub it in. It is also a highly effective tick repellent for dogs.

Rose geranium lemonade

Makes 1.5 litres (51 fl oz/6 cups)

Capture the citrusy tang of rose geranium
in an old-fashioned lemonade. Rose geranium
leaves are abundant all year round so you can
make this delicious lemonade any time you like.

115 g (4 oz/½ cup) caster (superfine) sugar
125 ml (4 fl oz/½ cup) freshly squeezed lemon juice
8 rose geranium leaves
ice cubes, to serve
rose geranium flowers, to garnish

Start by making a syrup. Combine the sugar with
500 ml (17 fl oz/2 cups) water in a saucepan and
bring to the boil. Remove from the heat and add
the geranium leaves, then cover and leave to infuse
for 30 minutes.

Strain the syrup through a fine-mesh sieve into a
jug, ready to serve. Stir in the lemon juice and 1 litre
(34 fl oz/4 cups) still or sparkling water. Add more
lemon juice to taste if required, then refrigerate
until needed.

To serve, top the lemonade with ice cubes and
stir through some rose geranium flowers.

Nasturtium flower pizza dough

Makes two 26 cm (10¼ in) pizza bases

This is a really impressive-looking pizza dough,
and the combination of nasturtium flowers, pesto and
goat's cheese adds to its sophisticated flavour.

1 tablespoon olive oil, plus extra for greasing
1 tablespoon dried yeast
1 teaspoon sea salt flakes
400 g (14 oz/2⅔ cups) plain (all-purpose) flour, plus
  extra for dusting
10 g (¼ oz/1 cup) nasturtium flowers

Combine the oil and 250 ml (8½ fl oz/1 cup)
lukewarm water in a jug or small bowl. Add the dry
ingredients to the bowl of a stand mixer fitted with
the dough hook attachment. Add the oil mixture and
nasturtium flowers to the dry ingredients and mix
until well combined. Turn out the dough and knead
on a lightly floured surface for 5–10 minutes, or until
the dough is smooth and elastic.

Place the dough in a clean bowl that has been lightly
greased with olive oil. Cover with a clean tea towel
(dish towel) or plastic wrap and leave to rise for
1½ hours. Tip the dough onto a lightly floured surface
and knock it back by punching the air out of it. Fold
the dough in half, then in half again and return to the
bowl. Cover and leave to rise for a further 30 minutes.

To make your pizza, cut the dough in half and
spread each piece of dough over a baking tray. Top
with your chosen toppings (I personally love olive oil,
pesto, feta cheese and nasturtium flowers) and bake
at 220°C (430°F) for 20–25 minutes.

*Note: If you don't have a stand mixer, combine the dry
ingredients and nasturtium flowers directly on a clean
work surface and create a well in the centre. Pour in
the oil and water mixture and begin to work the flour
in from the edges until well combined. Knead the dough
for 10–15 minutes until elastic and smooth, then continue
with the recipe.*

Nasturtium flower vinegar

Makes 500 ml (17 fl oz/2 cups)

Flower vinegars are really useful for any number
of savoury dishes. They can be used in marinades
for meat and seafood, to make a vinaigrette or simply
drizzled over a salad. I have used nasturtium in this
recipe, but rose petals, chive flowers, hibiscus or rose
geraniums would also work.

500 ml (17 fl oz/2 cups) white-wine vinegar
20 g (¾ oz/2 cups) freshly picked nasturtium flowers

Put the vinegar in a saucepan over medium heat and
simmer for 5 minutes, until warm.

Place the nasturtium flowers in a jar with a tight-
fitting lid and pour the warm vinegar over the flowers.
Seal the jar tightly and leave in direct sunlight for
up to 1 week to extract the colour and flavour from
the flowers.

Store in a cool, dry place for another week,
then strain the vinegar through a fine-mesh sieve into
a sterilised glass jar (see page 14), discarding
the flowers. The vinegar will keep indefinitely.

Use this nasturtium vinegar (left) whenever you need to add a pop of bright, peppery flavour to a dish.

NASTURTIUM

Trapaeoleum

Nasturtium is probably the most well-known edible flower, a fact which has probably taken focus away from its other edible parts. In fact, every single part of this old-school variety is edible, with its leaves, stems and pods all retaining the characteristic peppery flavour that makes its flowers so sought after.

————————

Easy to grow and a prolific self-seeder, you will commonly find the plant rambling out somewhere in the wild. Despite its weed-like growing habits, it is a staple ingredient in many restaurant dishes, appearing on menus in the form of green mousse, delicate young leaf foliage or pickled seed heads.

————————

The nasturtium is part of the cress family, which includes such varieties as watercress and land cress (all known for their peppery bite). All are true gardening companions, but the nasturtium is top dog, attracting pollinators and predators alike, as well as luring snails and slugs under its protective canopies and away from more sensitive plants.

Nutritional value

Flowers are high in both vitamin C and iron. The leaves also have a high concentration of vitamin C as well as antibiotic properties, which are at their most potent just before the plant begins to flower.

Origin

Native to South and Central America.

Favourite variety

Black Flame.

Seasonality / In the garden

Best grown from seed, nasturtiums are an easygoing variety that like full sun and tolerate partial shade. Although frost-tender, nasturtiums are hardy and will reward you with lush green leaves through the winter followed by plentiful flowers as the weather warms up. If left to their own devices, they will reappear in the same spot year after year.

Flavour pairings

Its tart flavour makes nasturtium perfect for savoury dishes, such as seafood and Asian-inspired food.

Did you know?

Its name is derived from Latin and means 'nose twist' (*nas* for nose and *tortum* for twist). The flower's spicy flavour makes even the untwitchiest nose twist.

What else you can do with it?

Nasturtiums have plenty of centuries-old medicinal uses. They are popular in herbal medicine as an antiseptic, used for treating chesty coughs and also to promote the formation of new blood cells.

Poor man's capers (pickled nasturtium seeds)

Makes 500 ml (17 fl oz/2 cups)

Harvest young, light green, half-ripened seed pods on the vine for this recipe. Young pods are crisp and juicy, but tend to lose their zip and flavour as they mature, eventually drying out into wrinkled brown seeds before dropping to the ground.

The raw seeds are full of potent mustard oils that give them a strong bitter flavour; a little too strong for most people's liking, so start by mellowing them out in a simple salty brine overnight.

Nasturtium capers have a nose-tingling bite that pairs well with spicy dishes, such as Asian stir-fries and sushi rolls. To use them, spoon out a few seeds and chop them up finely. You can add them to any dish that calls for traditional capers, such as pastas, sauces, salads and dressings. Just remember that a little goes a long way!

20 g (¾ oz/⅔ cup) nasturtium seed pods
80 g (2¾ oz/¼ cup) coarse sea salt
170 ml (5½ fl oz/⅔ cup) white vinegar (5 per cent acidity)
1 teaspoon caster (superfine) sugar
1 dried bay leaf

Remove the seeds from the pods and give them a quick rinse under cold running water to remove any dirt.

Combine the salt with 500 ml (17 fl oz/2 cups) water in a jar and stir until the salt has dissolved.

Add the nasturtium seeds, then place a zip-lock bag over the rim, pushing the bag down into the jar to keep the seeds submerged. Leave the seeds to brine for a couple of days at room temperature. During this stage, the seeds will turn a dull green colour. Strain the seeds through a fine-mesh sieve and rinse again to remove excess salt.

Combine the vinegar and sugar in a small saucepan over medium–high heat and bring to a low boil for 1 minute, stirring until the sugar has dissolved.

Divide the seeds between two sterilised 250 ml (8½ fl oz/1 cup) glass jars (see page 14) then pour the hot vinegar over the seeds, covering them completely. Leave the jars to cool at room temperature before sealing tightly. Store at room temperature or in the refrigerator. The pickled seeds will keep indefinitely in the vinegar.

Rose geranium leaf pound cake

Serves 10–12

This is an old-fashioned cake that is given a wonderful twist with the addition of heavily-scented rose geranium leaves. Pressing the leaves to the sides of the Bundt tin gives a fantastic visual effect.

500 g (1 lb 2 oz/2 cups) unsalted butter, plus extra for greasing
515 g (1 lb 2 oz/2¼ cups) caster (superfine) sugar
4 large organic, free-range eggs
2 teaspoons vanilla extract
zest of ½ a lemon
18–22 rose geranium leaves (10–12 torn and bruised, the rest left whole for lining the tin)
450 g (1 lb/3 cups) plain (all-purpose) flour, plus extra for dusting
pinch of salt
1 teaspoon bicarbonate of soda (baking soda)
250 ml (8½ fl oz/1 cup) buttermilk
1 tablespoon vegetable oil
icing (confectioners') sugar, for dusting
rose geranium flowers and small leaves, to garnish

Preheat the oven to 165°C (325°F) degrees. Grease a large ring (Bundt) tin and dust with flour.

Cream the butter and sugar together in a bowl until light and fluffy. Beat in the eggs, one at a time, then add the vanilla, lemon zest and torn rose geranium leaves, and mix until combined.

In a separate bowl, combine the flour, a pinch of salt and the bicarbonate of soda. Alternate adding the dry ingredients and the buttermilk to the butter and sugar mixture, being sure to start and finish with the dry ingredients.

Put the vegetable oil in a small bowl and briefly dip the remaining rose geranium leaves into the oil to coat. (This will make them adhere to the tin.)

Stick the oiled leaves in a pattern on the inside of the tin, pressing firmly to keep them in place.

Carefully pour in the mixture (try to prevent any mixture running between the leaves and the tin) and bake for 1 hour and 10 minutes, or until a skewer inserted in the middle of the cake comes out clean. Leave to cool completely in the pan before turning out and dusting with icing sugar. Decorate with rose geranium flowers and small leaves.

If you like, serve this moist Bundt cake (left) with a dollop of fresh cream or crème fraîche on the side.

CHRYSANTHEMUM

Chrysanthemum (asteraceae family)

The unofficial autumnal Mother's Day flower in Australia, the chrysanthemum is most commonly thought of as an ornamental plant for its showy flower heads. We usually display them in a vase, but in Asian cultures, the flowers, leaves and stems go straight to the kitchen where they are used in all manner of dishes.

In some parts of Asia, the yellow and white flowers from the species *Chrysanthemum morifolium* are boiled to make a tea known simply as chrysanthemum tea (or *júhuā chá* in Mandarin). In Chinese cuisine, the leaves, which have a slightly mustardy flavour and crispy texture, are simply boiled and used as steamed greens. The flowers are added to broths, including a snake meat soup, to enhance flavour. In Korea, a rice wine called gukhwaju is made from chrysanthemum flowers.

The natural insecticide pyrethrum is made from chrysanthemums. Active components extracted from the flowers are called pyrethrins, which attack the central nervous system of some insects. What's great about this insecticide is that it's not persistent, meaning it isn't toxic to mammals and birds like most synthetic insecticides. It's also biodegradable and will decompose easily with exposure to light.

Over fifty different species of chrysanthemum exist and are related to the daisy family, along with dahlias, sunflowers, marigolds, zinnias and cosmos. Native to East Asia, the Garland Chrysanthemum (also known as Shingiku in Japan and Tong Hao in China) is packed with vitamins that offer a multitude of health benefits.

Garland Chrysanthemums are rich in chlorogenic acid, which assists with weight loss by slowing the release of glucose into the bloodstream after a meal.

Nutritional value

High in antioxidants, fibre and chlorogenic acid, chrysanthemums are considered great for general health and weight loss. Rich in carotene, flavanoids, vitamins and potassium, they are also said to protect against cardiovascular disease and reduce the risk of lung cancer.

Origin

Native to Asia and northeast Europe.

Favourite variety

Garland

Seasonality / In the garden

Chrysanthemums typically flower in autumn and will grow in a variety of different soils. They must be propagated from either root divisions or cuttings and, with some full sun and good drainage, they will reward you with gorgeous blooms from late summer to the end of autumn.

Did you know?

NASA conducted a clean air study that showed chrysanthemum plants can reduce indoor air pollution.

Chrysanthemum leaf salad

Serves 2

This is a wonderful crisp and simple salad with a nod to Asian cuisine.

1 cos (romaine) lettuce
40 g (1½ oz/2 cups) chrysanthemum leaves
sea salt
fresh chrysanthemum flower florets, to garnish

Dressing
2 cm (¾ in) piece of ginger, peeled and chopped finely
½ tablespoon sesame oil
1 tablespoon grapeseed oil (you can also use peanut oil for a full-bodied flavour)
½ tablespoon rice-wine vinegar

To prepare the dressing, combine all the ingredients in a jar, seal tightly, and shake to combine. Set aside.

To make the salad, discard the green tips of the cos lettuce and roughly chop the heart and firmer white parts. In a salad bowl, toss the lettuce and chrysanthemum leaves together with the dressing.

Season with sea salt to taste and garnish with chrysanthemum flower florets.

Flower petal pasta

Makes 500 g (1 lb 2 oz)

This is a stunning, theatrical take on home-made pasta. Try a single variety of edible flower petals, like calendula or rose, or a mixture of varieties for a confetti pasta.

Small, flat petals are best suited to making pasta, and hand-cut pappardelle will give the best visual effect. You can replace the flower petals with fresh herbs or leaves if you prefer.

300 g (10½ oz/2 cups) tipo 00 flour, plus extra for dusting
2 large organic, free-range eggs
edible flower petals, such as calendula, nasturtium or dianthus petals, or cornflower florets

Place the flour on a clean work surface and make a well in the centre.

Beat the eggs with a fork in a small bowl and pour into the well. Using your hands, gently bring the flour in from the sides until the mixture is well blended and no longer sticky. If the mixture is too dry, add some water, a little at a time, to get the right consistency.

Flour your work surface and knead the dough using the palm of your hand. Once the dough is smooth and elastic, form it into a ball and transfer it to an oiled bowl. Cover with plastic wrap and refrigerate for 30 minutes.

Divide the dough into four and form small balls. Take one dough ball and flatten it with the palm of your hand.

With your pasta machine set to the largest setting, begin feeding the pasta through the machine. Fold the pasta dough in half between each setting. Once you have reached the second-last setting, arrange a quarter of the flower petals over half of the pasta sheet. Fold the other half over and lightly press down to enclose the petals. Feed the sheet through the pasta machine once more, then cut your pasta into the desired shape and set aside on a baking tray dusted with plenty of flour. Repeat with the remaining dough and petals.

If you'd prefer to dry the pasta, see page 28.

Roasted beetroot salad with fennel and anise hyssop

Serves 4 as an entrée

The earthiness of the roasted beetroot is offset by the sharp aniseed tang of the fennel and anise hyssop in this recipe. This is a great salad to serve as a side dish with marinated and barbecued meat, or something really savoury like roast pork.

500 g (1 lb 2 oz) heirloom beetroot
2 tablespoons olive oil
fresh thyme sprigs
1 fennel bulb
¼ red onion
¼ teaspoon caster (superfine) sugar
60 ml (2 fl oz/¼ cup) apple-cider vinegar
1 teaspoon sunflower oil, plus extra for drizzling
sea salt and freshly ground black pepper
50 g (1¾ oz) blue cheese, crumbled, to garnish
large handful of anise hyssop flowers and small leaves,
   to garnish

Preheat the oven to 190°C (375°F).
   Toss the beetroot with the olive oil, thyme sprigs and some salt and pepper in a bowl. Line a baking tray with foil and spread the beetroots on top. Bake for 45 minutes, or until the beetroot is tender when pierced with a sharp knife. Leave to cool, then peel the beetroot and cut into 5 cm (2 in) thick slices.
   Trim the fennel and finely shave it on a mandoline, discarding the white core. Finely julienne the onion and add to a bowl with the sugar, apple-cider vinegar, oil and some salt and pepper. Leave to macerate for 5 minutes, then combine with the shaved fennel and set aside.
   To serve, arrange the sliced beetroot on four plates (or use a single platter for a sharing dish) and season with salt and pepper and a drizzle of sunflower oil. Top with the shaved fennel and macerated onion, then garnish with a slice of blue cheese and a generous scattering of anise hyssop flowers and leaves.

ANISE HYSSOP

Agastache foeniculum

As the name suggests, anise hyssop has a sweet aniseed flavour and fragrance. A hardy perennial growing to almost 1 m (3.2 ft) high, it is a native wildflower of north-central North America. It is often mistaken as part of the anise (*Pimpinella anisum*) or hyssop (*Hyssopus officinalis*) families but, in fact, it belongs to an entirely different family; the mint family. The name anise hyssop stems from its sensory characteristics; an anise-like scent and flavour and flowers that appear similar to those of the true hyssop plant. It is also known as liquorice mint, blue giant hyssop, fragrant giant hyssop and lavender giant hyssop.

The lilac-coloured blooms of anise hyssop form dense spikes of tiny two-lipped flowers and have pointed, slightly furry leaves that are similar to catnip, which is also a member of the mint family. It is gorgeous when used as a perennial border in your herb garden and is a great pollinator; bees absolutely love it!

Anise hyssop is a great substitute for fresh mint. The flavour of the leaves is cooling in summer drinks and both the flowers and leaves can be used in salads and fruit salads. The gorgeous lilac flowers add a beautiful finish to sweet and savoury dishes with a slight liquorice flavour. You can also use the dried leaves as an accompaniment to lamb, chicken, oily fish like salmon and with some vegetables where mint would work, like peas.

Nutritional value

Anise hyssop is high in antioxidants and, as an essential oil, it has antiviral, antibacterial and anti-inflammatory properties. The compound limonene, also present in anise hyssop, has been found to neutralise stomach acid and promote a healthy digestive tract.

Origin

North-central North America.

Favourite variety

Common anise hyssop.

Seasonality/In the garden

Anise hyssop can either be started from seed indoors or you can purchase seedlings from specialty nurseries. Once established, anise hyssop has a sucker growing habit, which means more plants will sprout from its root growth. It will thrive and spread in a warm sunny position and is tolerant of most soils, including poor to clay-rich soils. Best pruned back by 50 per cent at the end of the flowering season, flowers will bloom from summer to autumn and its fragrant foliage can be harvested year-round.

Culinary uses/Flavour profiles

Aniseed and sweet liquorice flavours make anise hyssop the ideal culinary herb for infusions, cocktails and desserts. It can also be used in teas, rice dishes, with pork and is great with stone fruit and berries. Steep sprigs of anise hyssop in milk or cream for panna cotta, custards or ice cream. It also pairs well with chocolate.

What else you can do with it?

Anise hyssop is a great companion plant to herbs such as garlic chives, oregano and thyme. It was also used medicinally by Native Americans to treat coughs, fever, wounds and diarrhoea.

CUCURBITS

Cucurbitaceae

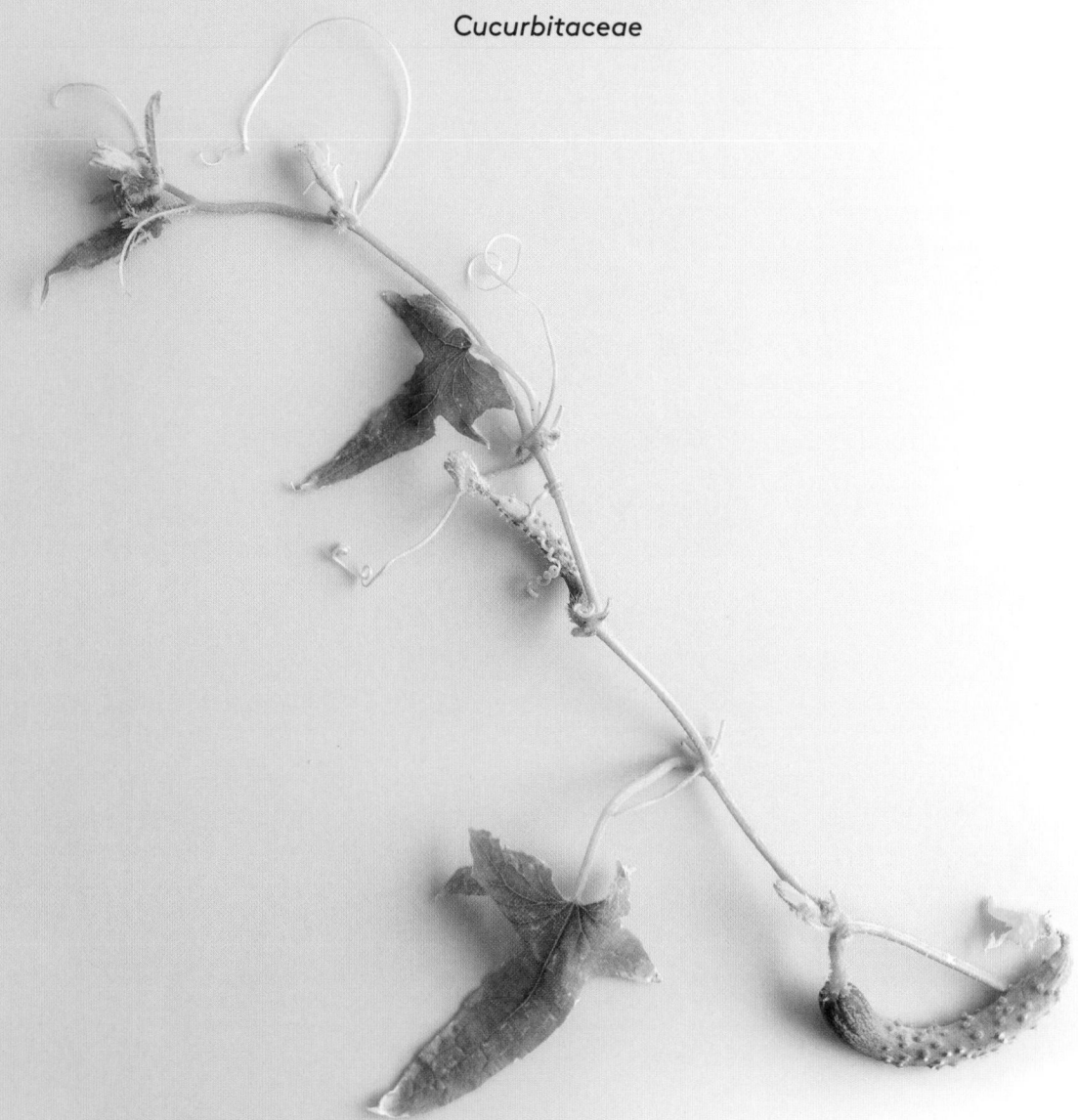

Cucurbits are a family of vegetables that produce our largest yield of food for human consumption. It includes pumpkin, squash, cucumber and melons. No doubt this statistic may have something to do with the weight and size of cucurbit fruit – after all, a single pumpkin can grow to over 1 tonne – but it is also due to the 1,000+ varieties in the family.

———————

These are some of our oldest domesticated vegetables. The cucumber, for example, dates back as early as 7,750 BC, originating in south-east Asia. More recently, Roman Emperor Tiberius considered the plant so important that he had cucumbers grown in mobile carts so they could be moved to capture maximum sunlight.

———————

Made up of 90 per cent water and with flesh that stays several degrees cooler than the outside air temperature, it's no surprise that the cucumber has always been regarded as a cooling fruit, used to treat burns and quench thirst.

While it's the fruit of this family that are the most prized, its flowers are also sizeable and prolific, making them appealing for use in cooking. It is not unusual to see seasonal blossoms from zucchini (courgette) and pumpkin plants on a menu, however what isn't so commonplace is the use of the foliage, which is typically coarse and riddled with spikes. Instead, it's the tender young greens, specifically the shoots, that are best to use, and they have a similar flavour and nutrient profile to spinach. By picking these growth tips off the plant you will also help refocus growing energy towards the fruit on the vine.

Nutritional value

A good source of potassium and vitamin A, the cucurbit family is high in dietary fibre and low in calories. Zucchini is a rich source of manganese and vitamin C and also contains magnesium, folate, potassium, copper and phosphorus. One cup of pumpkin will provide us with 20–30 per cent of our daily requirement of vitamin A.

Origin

Native to North America.

Favourite variety

Spaghetti squash.

Seasonality/In the garden

Cucurbits produce both male and female flowers, with fruit formed from pollinated female flowers. Most of this work is done by honey bees in the early morning when the short-lived flowers appear. Easily grown from seed, cucurbits need fertile, compost-rich, well-drained soil and full sun. Pumpkins are excellent ground-cover plants and varieties like the cucumber will happily grow up a trellis.

Sautéed pumpkin leaves with peanut butter

Serves 2

Pumpkin leaves, and those of other cucurbits, are not often considered as ingredients in their own right. They are however plentiful, full of nutrition and have a strong spinach flavour.

This dish uses peanut butter, but if you suffer from a nut allergy, you can easily replace the peanut butter with a seed butter or tahini, or leave it out altogether and bulk out the dish with extra tomatoes.

Before cooking with pumpkin leaves it's important to know how to prepare them by stripping their spikes. Break part of the upper stem and pull the spiky strings all the way down, including from the leaf foliage. It's similar to de-stringing celery, and it's immensely satisfying.

1 bunch pumpkin leaves
1 teaspoon sea salt
1 teaspoon bicarbonate of soda (baking soda; optional)
1 tablespoon coconut oil
1 onion, finely diced
1 tomato, diced
2–3 tablespoons peanut butter

Wash the pumpkin leaves well under cold running water to remove any grit, then strip the stems and leaves of spikes. Finely chop the leaves.

Combine 125 ml (4 fl oz/½ cup) boiling water and the salt in a saucepan over low–medium heat and add the pumpkin leaves. The leaves tend to lose their colour when cooked, so add a teaspoon of bicarbonate of soda if desired to help keep them vibrant green. Cover and leave for 3–4 minutes, until wilted. Once wilted, drain and set aside.

Melt the coconut oil in a saucepan over medium heat and fry the onion for 2–3 minutes, until softened. Add the tomato and fry for another 2 minutes, then add the peanut butter and stir to combine. Mix in the pumpkin leaves, reduce the heat to low and simmer for 5–10 minutes.

Beer-battered stuffed zucchini flowers

Makes 12–16

This dish is ideal if you find yourself with plenty of zucchini flowers but not much fruit. Depending on your taste, these can be made using a beer or tempura batter, and you can play around with the stuffing too. The key is eating them as soon as your mouth can bear the heat; letting them go soggy would be the ultimate sin, so prepare these guys just before serving.

12–16 fresh zucchini (courgette) flowers
vegetable oil, for deep-frying, approx. 500 ml
  (17 fl oz/2 cups) depending on the size of your pan

Stuffing
200 g (7 oz) fresh ricotta
100 g (3½ oz) goat's cheese
1 garlic clove, finely chopped
handful of fresh flat-leaf (Italian) parsley, chopped
½ red onion, finely chopped
handful of freshly grated parmesan
sea salt and freshly ground black pepper

Beer batter
125 g (4½ oz/1 cup) cornflour (cornstarch)
150 g (5½ oz/1 cup) self-raising flour
1 x 330 ml (11 fl oz) bottle beer (approx.; see method)
150 g (5½ oz/1 cup) plain (all-purpose) flour,
  for dusting
sea salt

To make the stuffing, combine all the ingredients in a bowl and season to taste with salt and pepper.

Remove the stamens from the zucchini flowers, leaving the stem intact. Roll up balls of the stuffing and place them inside the flowers (you can also use a piping/icing bag to pipe the filling into the flowers). Gently twist the petals at the top to seal the stuffing inside.

To make the beer batter, combine the cornflour and self-raising flour in a bowl and stir in enough beer to make a mixture that is sticky but not runny. Add the plain flour to another bowl.

Heat the vegetable oil in a deep, heavy-based saucepan over medium–high heat until it reaches 180°C (350°F) on a cooking thermometer.

Working one at a time, dip the zucchini flowers first in the flour then in the beer batter. Deep-fry the zucchini flowers in the hot oil, in batches if necessary to avoid overcrowding the pan, until they are golden and crisp. Season generously with sea salt and serve on a bed of crisp green leaves or on their own as a canapé.

BLACKCURRANT

Ribes nigrum

Containing four times the vitamin C of oranges and twice the antioxidants of blueberries, the humble blackcurrant is a nutrition powerhouse. It even beats exotic fruits like the goji berry, long thought to have offered the best health benefits.

Fruits that have a deep purple or red colour perform well on the antioxidant scale, where the darkest fruits contain the highest antioxidant content. With its deep purple-black berries, blackcurrant is now being heralded as the ultimate 'superfruit' that can help prevent cancer, Alzheimer's, heart disease and diabetes.

Released in 1975, modern varieties from the 'Ben' series such as 'Ben Sarek', 'Ben Connan', 'Ben Hope' and 'Ben Lomond' were developed in Europe to be more productive and disease- and frost-tolerant. The fruiting habit of traditional varieties was not suitable for the juicing industry as the bunches naturally fruit in succession from the base, meaning the fruit ripens unevenly. These modern varieties ripen in even, whole bunches making harvesting faster and more predictable.

Blackcurrants can be eaten raw but are usually cooked in a variety of sweet and savoury dishes. Tart in flavour, you can use them in pies and jams, jellies, syrups and even to make Cassis, a blackcurrant liqueur.

Nutritional value

Very high in vitamin C and polyphenol antioxidants, which improves blood circulation. Blackcurrants also help to reduce inflammation and boost the immune system.

Origin

Northern Europe and northern Asia.

Favourite variety

Ben Sarek.

Seasonality/In the garden

Blackcurrants are easy to grow. Like most fruiting trees and shrubs, bare-rooted stock can be planted in winter in well-drained soil with a little compost and in a sunny position. They are also great container plants and will tolerate most soil types. In mid-summer your plant will produce bunches of dark purple to black fruit.

Historical fact

French monks produced blackcurrant liqueur for medicinal use, including the treatment of snakebites.

Did you know?

During World War Two, many vitamin C-rich fruits, such as oranges, became unavailable in the UK. To meet the wartime demand for vitamin-rich foods, national crop levels of blackcurrant were rapidly increased and made into blackcurrant syrup that was distributed free of charge to children under the age of two.

Cream of blackcurrant leaves

Serves 4

500 g (1 lb 2 oz) caster (superfine) sugar
40 g (1½ oz/1½ cups) blackcurrant leaves, loosely
  packed
juice of 3 lemons
250 ml (8½ fl oz/1 cup) thick (double/heavy) cream,
  whipped
fresh blackcurrants, to garnish

Combine the sugar with 250 ml (8½ fl oz/1 cup) water
in a saucepan and bring to the boil. Reduce the heat to
medium, add the blackcurrant leaves and simmer for
15 minutes. Remove from the heat and leave to cool.

Strain the syrup through a fine-mesh sieve into
a bowl. Stir in the lemon juice and cream.

Divide the mixture between four serving glasses and
chill until needed. Garnish with fresh blackcurrants.

Blackcurrant sorbet

Serves 4

200 g (7 oz) golden caster (superfine) sugar
20 g (¾ oz) fresh mint, plus small sprigs to serve
750 g (1 lb 11 oz) fresh blackcurrants
4 tablespoons liquid glucose
juice of 2 lemons

Start by making a syrup. Combine the sugar with
200 ml (7 fl oz) boiling water in a bowl, stirring to
dissolve the sugar. Add the mint and leave to infuse
for about 15 minutes, or until the syrup is cool.

Remove the mint and transfer the syrup to a
medium saucepan. Add the blackcurrants and liquid
glucose and simmer over medium heat for about
5 minutes, stirring regularly to ensure the syrup
doesn't catch. Once the fruit has softened, transfer
the mixture to a food processor and pulse to combine.
Strain through a fine-mesh sieve into a bowl and stir
in lemon juice. Set aside to cool.

If you have an ice-cream maker:

Freeze according to manufacturer's instructions
until it reaches a thick, slushy consistency, then scoop
into an airtight container and freeze.

If you don't have an ice-cream maker:

Pour into a shallow airtight container and freeze.
Whisk the mixture 3 or 4 times as it freezes to stop
ice crystals forming.

Remove the sorbet from the freezer a few minutes
before serving to allow the sorbet to soften slightly.
Garnish with small sprigs of fresh mint.

Rumtopf

Makes 4 kg (8 lb 13 oz)

Rumtopf, also known as bachelor's jam, is not really a jam at all. It's more like a cocktail of rum-soaked fruit! The idea is that you gradually add fruit, alcohol and sugar to create a mixture as different fruits ripen throughout the season. This preserve is usually prepared for Christmas, when the potent fruity alcohol is drunk and the highly-spirited fruit can be served on its own or with ice cream and puddings. You don't have to use rum either; brandy, vodka or gin all make wonderful boozy brews.

To make the rumtopf, you will need a large glazed stoneware or earthenware pot with a tight-fitting lid, and a small plate, saucer or other flat object that will fit inside the pot and keep the fruit submerged.

2 kg (4 lb 6 oz) summer fruit, such as strawberries, cherries, peaches, apricots, pears, blood orange, grapes or pineapple
2 litres (68 fl oz/8 cups) rum, brandy, vodka or gin (40 per cent ABV)
1 kg (2 lb 3 oz) caster (superfine) sugar

Choose just-ripe fruit as it begins to appear through the summer and autumn, ideally starting off your rumtopf with the first small, sweet strawberries of the season.

Place the fruit in the bottom of your pot and, for every 500 g (1 lb 2 oz) fruit, sprinkle over 250 g (9 oz) sugar. Mix, then leave for 1 hour to macerate.

Pour in about 1 litre (34 fl oz/4 cups) of your chosen alcohol, place the saucer on top of the fruit, then cover the mouth of the pot with plastic wrap and seal with the lid.

Continue adding fruit, sugar and alcohol throughout the summer and autumn, ensuring the alcohol always covers the fruit by 2 cm (¾ in). Do not stir the fruit at any point. When the pot is full, seal it tightly and leave for 1–2 months at room temperature to allow the flavours to mature.

Just before serving, give the contents a good stir to combine everything. Use within 12 months.

Citrus leaf chilli paste

Makes approx. 1 x 250 ml (8½ fl oz/1 cup) jar

A few years ago, we did a magical contra deal that involved this spicy, citrusy, mouth-pounding sauce. We supplied the fresh chillies – which we were growing in abundance on our rooftop garden – and a friendly Indonesian man provided this recipe. Apparently, his mother-in-law was due to arrive in a matter of days and, not wanting to disappoint, he needed a few crucial ingredients. One of them was lemon leaf, which he wasn't likely to find in a supermarket or overhanging his balcony in the CBD.

We'd always been familiar with kaffir lime leaf and how it added a real floral note to dishes, but little did we know that lemon foliage, or orange or grapefruit for that matter, would work just as well.

10–15 chillies, finely chopped (whichever variety you prefer)
2–3 shallots, finely diced
3 garlic cloves, chopped
3 teaspoons palm sugar (jaggery)
1 teaspoon chopped fresh galangal
2 teaspoons shrimp paste
2 tablespoons olive oil
2 lemongrass stems, cut into 4 pieces
6–8 lemon leaves, finely sliced
sea salt

Combine the chilli, shallot, garlic, sugar, galangal, shrimp paste and 1 tablespoon olive oil in a mortar and mix with a pestle until combined.

Heat the remaining oil in a frying pan and sauté the paste and lemongrass stems for 4–5 minutes.

Add the sliced lemon leaves and a couple of tablespoons of water and simmer gently until the water evaporates and the paste thickens.

Remove the lemongrass stems and season the paste with salt. Transfer the paste to a sterilised glass jar (see page 14), ready for adding to soups, stir-fries and curries.

CITRUS

Rutaceae

My first memory of a citrus tree was as a small girl falling off my grandmother's back step into her cumquat bush. On reflection, I think my big brother may have pushed me, but either way I can still remember how much the cumquat bush's thorny stems grazed and hurt my small limbs and how my grandmother appeased me with her secret stash of lollies.

To many of us, citrus trees hold firm and fond memories of our childhoods, whether it was a lemon tree in the backyard or a bag of oranges from a neighbour who had a glut of fruit. In the 1980s, my mother planted a small Meyer lemon in a pot at home. It produced such sweet and reliable fruit for a good part of the year. When I moved out of home in my twenties we bought what seemed so exotic at the time: a Tahitian lime tree that yielded nicely in time for summer gin and tonics.

When buying citrus fruits at the supermarket, it's often a difficult proposition. They tend to be very expensive and we often end up purchasing fruit out of season that has been imported from California. Citrus fruits are so easy to grow, it seems silly not to be growing them in our gardens at home. Citrus varieties are perfect for use as ornamental or landscaping trees, and the bonus is they produce wonderful fruit to be picked. You needn't have a large garden; citrus happily grow in pots and are commonly espaliered as a screen against a fence or wall. They also create a great evergreen hedge that will flower and fruit throughout the year.

Nutritional value

Citrus are most commonly known for their high vitamin C content; good for strengthening the immune system.

They help improve skin elasticity and are rich in vitamins and minerals such as vitamin B, potassium, phosphorous, copper and magnesium that are all essential to assist your body's ability to function properly.

Origin

Native to Asia and the Malay Archipelago.

Favourite variety

Yuzu

Seasonality/In the garden

Subtropical plants like citrus trees actually grow very well in cooler-climate cities as high-density urban environments are full of heat-retaining surfaces like bitumen and high-rise architecture that helps to ward off frosts.

Lemons, limes and oranges will commonly fruit from winter through to early summer, but there are also varieties, such as finger limes and the lemonade tree, that will reward you with fruit in the height of summer through to early autumn.

Other varieties

There are over fifty varieties of citrus that are commonly (and uncommonly) grown, but here is a list of some key and important species and hybrids to know:
Pomelo
Citron
Lemon
Tangerine
Mandarin orange
Bitter orange
Sweet orange
Papeda
Key lime

Candied orange rind

Makes 8 slices

115 g (4 oz/½ cup) caster (superfine) sugar
1 orange, cut into 5 mm (¼ in) slices

Combine the sugar with 375 ml (12½ fl oz/1½ cups) water in a saucepan and bring to the boil over medium heat. Add the sliced orange and simmer for about 20 minutes, turning occasionally, until the liquid has reduced to a thin syrup and the orange slices are translucent.

Reduce the heat to low and simmer for a further 10 minutes, or until the syrup is thick and the slices are tender but still intact. Transfer the orange slices to a wire rack to cool. Store the leftover syrup in an airtight container in the refrigerator and use to drizzle over desserts or breakfast hotcakes.

Citron rind salad

(Insalata di cedro)
Serves 2

The elusive citron is a little misunderstood. With very little juice and a spongy pith making up 70 per cent of its fruit, many would consider it inedible, but its sweet pith and scented, bitter rind are great in food and drinks. You can make a simple syrup with the leftover pulp by boiling it with equal parts water and caster sugar for 10 minutes. Or use the rind to make a citron-based liqueur (a bit like limoncello) called cedrello.

1 x 500 g (1 lb 2 oz) citron
1 red onion
handful of flat-leaf (Italian) parsley
1 teaspoon salted capers, rinsed and soaked in water
   10 minutes
juice of 2 lemons
100 ml (3½ fl oz) extra-virgin olive oil
sea salt and freshly ground black pepper

Peel the citron rind using a vegetable peeler, being sure to keep the slices of thick white rind free of any peel or pulp. Cut the citron into quarters and scoop out the pulp using a paring knife, then finely slice the rind.

Finely slice the onion, roughly chop the parsley and capers, then combine the citron rind, parsley, onion and capers in a bowl.

For the dressing, whisk together the lemon juice and olive oil and toss through the salad. The rind is like a sponge, so make sure you dress the salad quickly to ensure everything is evenly coated. Allow the salad to sit for 1 hour before serving. Season to taste with salt and pepper.

My mother's cumquat marmalade

Makes 1.5 litres (51 fl oz/6 cups)

Maybe it's the tiny, bonsai-like fruit that makes cumquat marmalade feel like the most coveted of all marmalades, or it could be the fruit's uniquely tart flavour, but a replenishment of my mother's cumquat marmalade is always a welcome arrival in my house. 'Doodie's marmalade' is my son's breakfast of choice smothered over grainy toast, either enjoyed in his high chair or snatched from my plate.

1 kg (2 lb 3 oz) cumquats
2 tablespoons freshly squeezed lemon juice
1.15 kg (2½ lb/5 cups) caster (superfine) sugar

Wash and quarter the cumquats then place them in a non-metallic bowl. Pour in 1.25 litres (42 fl oz/5 cups) water, cover the bowl with plastic wrap and leave to stand overnight.

Transfer the water and cumquats to a large saucepan, stir in the lemon juice and bring to the boil over medium–high heat. Reduce the heat and simmer for 30 minutes, or until the cumquats have softened. Meanwhile, place a couple of saucers in the freezer to chill.

Add the sugar to the cumquats and stir until dissolved. Bring the jam back to the boil over high heat and boil uncovered, for 20 minutes, or until the jam has reached setting point. To test this, spoon a little jam onto a chilled saucer. Leave it for 1 minute then tip the saucer – if the surface of the jam wrinkles, or if a film pulls up when touched with a fingertip, the jam is ready. Remember to remove the pot from the heat while you test the jam to prevent it from overcooking.

When the jam has reached setting point, remove the pan from the heat and leave to stand for 10 minutes. Carefully scoop out any visible pips. Pour into sterilised glass jars (see page 14) and seal tightly.

Oysters wrapped in lemon leaves

Serves 2

When choosing lemon leaves, it is advisable to know their provenance. As the leaves are not commercially harvested, you want to make sure they haven't been sprayed with any chemicals, so try to pick them from your own or a local tree.

This recipe is a wonderful summertime appetiser. Serve it on a platter or as an entrée with some wedges of lemon. Perfect accompanied by a crisp white or sparkling wine.

12 fresh oysters, shucked
olive oil
handful of fresh breadcrumbs
handful of chopped mint
zest of 1 lemon
1 garlic clove, finely chopped
12 large organic lemon leaves, wiped clean
sea salt and freshly ground black pepper
lemon wedges, to serve

Remove the oysters from their shells and drizzle the oysters with a little olive oil. In a bowl, combine the breadcrumbs, mint, lemon zest, garlic and some salt and pepper. Roll each of the oysters in the breadcrumb mixture.

Place an oyster on a lemon leaf, roll it up and secure with a toothpick. Bake or grill on the barbecue for about 5 minutes, or until the oysters just start to sizzle.

Serve immediately with lemon wedges.

PRESERVING EDIBLE FLOWERS

Eating flowers is not a new concept. In medieval times, flowers were commonly used in an assortment of dishes, and many were credited for both their medicinal and magical properties.

As gardeners, it is drilled into us that it's a bad thing to let herbs and edible plants go to flower, but doing this allows you to benefit from every stage of a plant's life, and produces another exciting ingredient: the edible flower.

Before the days of refrigeration, humans preserved their food as a way of survival, bottling up many plants' nutrients for the colder months when food was scarce and the winters were long. There are many ways to preserve the bounty of summer, from drying and freezing, to steeping ingredients in alcohol and vinegar. Edible flowers can be cooked and crystallised, or preserved in jams and syrups.

What is so wonderful about preserving edible flowers though, is that cooking our blooms intensifies their incredible flavours and colours.

Flower ice blocks

Flower ice blocks are a fun and pretty way to finish your summer drinks. They are so easy to make, but do require a little pre-planning. The best bit is they last in the freezer for months!

small edible flowers or petals
water
ice-cube trays

Place a flower or petal in each ice-cube hole and half-fill with water. Freeze for 1 hour, or until ice begins to form, then fill the ice trays to the top. Leave to freeze completely before serving.

For larger ice blocks, fill trays with water and layered flowers, filling them up 1 cm (½ in) at a time, to create a layered look. Freeze for 1 hour between each layer.

Note: You can also add fresh herb leaves to the layered ice blocks to add interesting flavours.

Drying flowers

Drying flowers is a simple way to preserve the beauty of your garden long after the flowering season has ended. Although most flowers lose their colour once dried, some, like the cornflower, hold on to their former glory. To ensure the best colour, cut flowers just before they are fully open and opt for darker drying locations, because light can bleach the flowers. As a rule of thumb, blue and yellow flowers retain more of their colour when air-dried than pink blooms, which tend to fade.

Air-drying

This method is especially good for drying loose petals, flower heads and leaves, and the finished flowers look like they dried naturally. Air drying requires a flat surface that allows air to circulate around the flowers. You can use a window screen, drying trays, muslin that has been hung like a hammock, or newspaper laid flat on the floor.

To dry petals, spread them out on a flat surface in a single layer. For flower heads, place them in single-layer rows, heads facing up. To dry leaves with stems or single-stem flowers, lay them down in a random manner, but don't let them overlap.

The air-drying method takes anywhere from several days to weeks.

Oven-drying

Oven-drying flowers requires a controlled temperature of about 40–60°C (104–140°F) and can be used if you don't have the space to hang or air-dry, or if you need something dried quickly.

Preheat the oven to 40–60°C (104–140°F) and leave the door slightly ajar so that any lingering moisture can escape. Place the flowers in a single layer on a baking tray lined with baking paper.

Transfer to the oven, watching them carefully and turning them every 15 minutes. When the flowers are crisp and brittle, remove them from the oven.

Depending on what you are drying, this process can take anywhere from a few minutes to several hours.

Flower sugar

Makes approx. 230 g (8 oz/1 cup)

Sugar has been used as a preservative for thousands of years, especially in northern climates that lacked sufficient sunlight to dry food.

The height of summer, when flowers are plentiful and highly aromatic, is the ideal time to stock up and preserve your flowers. Flower sugar is a quick and easy way to bottle the heady scent of summer blooms and can be used in your baking year-round. Sprinkle the sugar over hotcakes, or use it to make cakes and desserts; it is very versatile. Violets and roses yield the best colours.

230 g (8 oz/1 cup) caster
  (superfine) sugar
15 g (½ oz/½ cup) fresh edible
  flower petals, stems removed

Place the sugar and flowers in a food processor and pulse for 2 minutes. Transfer the flower sugar to a sterilised glass jar (see page 14), seal tightly and store in a cool, dark place for up to 1 year.

Note: If you're using lavender, a few flower heads per 230 g (8 oz/1 cup) sugar is enough. When using violets, 2–3 tablespoons per 230 g (8 oz/ 1 cup) of sugar will suffice.

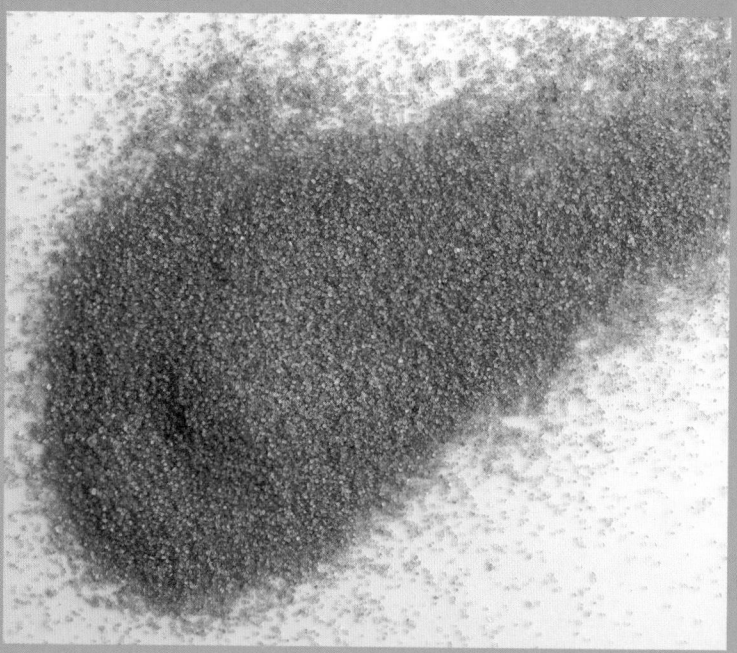

Strong-scented flowers like rose and violet are best for making flower sugar.

Spread this fragrant rose petal jam on toast, or use it to layer cakes.

Rose petal jam

Makes approx. 1 litre (34 fl oz/
4 cups)

I like to use pink or red roses for
natural colour in this recipe.

250 g (9 oz) fresh, fragrant rose
  petals, white tips trimmed
juice of 2 lemons
460 g (1 lb/2 cups) caster (superfine)
  sugar
50 g (1¾ oz) powdered fruit pectin

Toss the rose petals, lemon juice
and half the sugar together in a
bowl until the petals are evenly
coated. Cover with plastic wrap
and leave to stand at room
temperature overnight.
  Bring 750 ml (25½ fl oz/3 cups)
water to the boil in a saucepan over
medium heat. Add the remaining
sugar and rose petal mixture and
stir until the sugar has dissolved.
Reduce the heat to medium–low and
simmer for 20 minutes. Increase the
heat and boil the jam for 5 minutes.
Stir in the powdered pectin and boil
for another minute.
  Divide the jam between four
250 ml (8½ fl oz/1 cup) sterilised
glass jars (see page 14) and seal
tightly while the jam is still hot.
Store in a cool, dark place for 12–18
months and refrigerate once opened.

Rosewater

Makes 1 litre (34 fl oz/4 cups)

Your own home-grown distilled
rosewater will not only be far more
fragrant than the store-bought
variety, but if you use red roses,
it will colour the water a cheery
raspberry pink!

12 scented red rose heads, petals
  removed and stems discarded
ice cubes

You will need:
A saucepan with a lid (ideally
  a glass lid)
A small, heatproof bowl

Pick your roses just after they have
opened first thing in the morning
for optimal fragrance.
  Put the rose petals in a saucepan
and cover with 1 litre (34 fl oz/4
cups) water. Float a small, heatproof
bowl in the centre, being careful
not to splash any water into the
bowl. Cover with the lid upturned
and bring to the boil before reducing
the heat to a simmer.
  Once the water begins to condense
on the underside of the lid, place
a few ice cubes on the outside
of the lid to accelerate the distilling
process. You will need to soak up
the ice cubes as they melt. Inside
the pan, the water will condense
and drip into the bowl. This will
take about 1 hour.
  Lift the bowl out of the saucepan
and leave to cool, then transfer the
rose water to a 1 litre (34 fl oz/4 cup)
sterilised glass bottle (see page 14)
and store in the refrigerator for
up to 2 weeks.

Floral vodka

Makes 250 ml (8½ fl oz/1 cup)

This is a super easy method of
preserving and enjoying your edible
flowers. All kinds of flowers will
work, and you can use gin instead
of vodka if you like. Just be sure
to use only one kind of flower
in the infusion.

30 g (1 oz/1 cup) fresh edible flower
  petals, stems removed
250 ml (8½ fl oz/1 cup) vodka

Roughly chop the petals and place
them in a sterilised glass jar (see
page 14). Cover with the vodka, seal
the jar tightly and leave to macerate
in the refrigerator for a minimum
of 1 week. Strain the vodka through
a fine-mesh sieve into a sterilised
bottle or jar, discarding the flowers,
and store in the refrigerator or
freezer for up to 1 year.

*Note: You can use rose petals,
dianthus, dandelions, nasturtiums,
and tulips, to name a few. If you
are using elderflower, use 10 g
(¼ oz/½ cup) elderflowers for every
250 ml (8½ fl oz/1 cup) of vodka
and only 2 tablespoons of lavender
for every (8½ fl oz/1 cup) of vodka.*

Persian violet fairy floss

Makes approx. 1 kg (2 lb 3 oz)

1 kg (2 lb 3 oz) Flower sugar
  (page 168)
100 g (3½ oz) golden syrup or
  corn syrup
5 ml (¼ fl oz) white vinegar

You will also need:
A digital thermometer
olive oil
cornflour (cornstarch)
pliable rubber candy mould

Add the sugar, golden syrup and
white vinegar to a large saucepan,
followed by 500 ml (17 fl oz/2 cups)
water.

Place the saucepan over medium–
low heat and heat the mixture,
without stirring, until it reaches
133°C (271°F) on the thermometer.
This should take 20–25 minutes.
Use a wet pastry brush to wipe
any sugar crystals from the side
of the pan.

Remove from the heat and leave
to cool to 100°C (212°F). Pour the
mixture into the candy mould to
around 5 cm (2 in), then leave
to cool completely.

Gently (and patiently) squeeze
the candies out of their moulds.
Coat them in a little olive oil to stop
them sticking to your hands, then
carefully mould each candy into
an even doughnut shape.

Lightly dust a work surface with
cornflour, lay a candy doughnut
on the surface, and stretch it out
to 20 cm (8 in) long, dusting with
cornflour as you go. Fold it into a
figure of eight, then hold it in place
with one hand while you use the
other hand to tease out the strands.
Switch hands to ensure they're even
on both sides, ensuring the candy
always stays on the cornflour. Make
another figure of eight and repeat
with four strands. Repeat 14 times
in total and you will have over
16,000 tiny strands of fairy floss.

Cut into lengths as required
and serve tousled over desserts and
sweet dishes.

Violet toffee

Serves 2

460 g (1 lb/2 cups) violet sugar
  (see Flower sugar, page 168)
250 g (9 oz/1 cup) unsalted butter
2 tablespoons white vinegar
90 g (3 oz/¼ cup) golden syrup
  or corn syrup
¼ cup water

Combine all the ingredients with
60 ml (2 fl oz/¼ cup) water in
a large, heavy-based saucepan over
medium heat. Mix until the sugar
has dissolved, then bring to the boil
and do not stir until the mixture is
dark golden. To test the toffee, drop
a little into a glass of cold water; it's
ready when it hardens immediately.

Remove the pan from the heat and
pour the toffee onto a baking tray
lined with baking paper to a
1 cm (½ in) thickness. Leave to cool
and harden slightly, then score into
squares. When completely cool, use
a blunt instrument like a hammer
to break the squares apart. Store
in an airtight container at room
temperature for up to 6 weeks,
or store for up to 6 months in the
refrigerator.

Crystallised flowers

Makes 60 g (2 oz/2 cups)

These little gems are perfect for topping cakes and desserts. Not only does the sugar preserve the petals for up to 1 year, but the sugary crunch of their outer crust adds a whole new flavour dimension to your flowers. The fragrance of rose petals, viola or violets will bring new life to sweet treats.

1 organic, free-range egg white
460 g (1 lb/2 cups) caster (superfine) sugar
60 g (2 oz/2 cups) edible flowers, such as rose petals, violas and pansies

Whisk the egg white in a bowl until it is light and fluffy. Put the caster sugar in a food processor and pulse until it forms a fine powder.

Using a fine brush, paint the egg white onto the front and back of the flowers and petals, ensuring they are completely coated. Sprinkle the sugar evenly over the wet petals and transfer the flowers, face down, to a baking tray lined with baking paper.

Leave to dry for about 24 hours. The petals will harden as the egg white dries.

Store your crystallised flowers at room temperature in a sealed container lined with baking paper or tissue paper.

Making crystallised flowers (right) requires patience, but they are worth the effort. If you find they are going soggy, use a little less egg white.

Other flowers you can crystallise: Dianthus, cornflowers, lavender, pelargonium, primrose and violets.

NIGHTSHADES

Nightshades are a plant family, botanically known as *Solanaceae*, that include a number of our most popular vegetable varieties, such as tomatoes, capsicums and eggplants. They are so named because they do their growing in the shade of the night, rather than in the light of the sun.

Nearly all of the plants that belong to this family originated in the Altiplano region of South America near the Andes mountains, and were popularised in the fifteenth century by explorers travelling offshore. While the list of edible nightshades is small, the number of poisonous varieties is quite extensive.

Most nightshades are toxic to humans. The best-known of these is belladonna, or 'deadly nightshade', a poison around which the plot of Shakespeare's *Macbeth* revolves. It contains tropane alkaloids that cause hallucination and delirium, as well as trouble generating saliva and swallowing. A coma and convulsions usually precede death. Though the root is believed to have the highest concentration of the toxins, the edible-looking berries are usually the cause of accidental poisoning. Ingestion of a single leaf or about 15–20 of its berries can be fatal in adults. Ironically, the name 'belladonna' literally translates as beautiful woman in Italian, and it was so named because Venetian women used it to enlarge their pupils, which apparently increased their attractiveness.

Good use of poison?

The powerful poison of the deadly nightshade is now the source of the antispasmodic drug atropine, which is used to treat nerve agent and pesticide poisonings and to decrease saliva production during surgery.

Glycoalkaloids in edible nightshades

As a natural defence mechanism against pests and disease, all nightshades produce glycoalkaloids, which are bitter compounds found throughout the plant. The highest concentration of this compound can be found in the leaves, flowers, roots and unripe fruit. So, they are essentially designed to be toxic, to defend themselves against fungi, viruses and insects. Although typically not fatal to humans, the toxicity can still cause problems, particularly people that have digestive sensitivity or those struggling with an autoimmune disease. If consumed in small doses, symptoms may include vomiting and diarrhoea, whereas at higher doses, much more serious symptoms can occur, such as fever, low blood pressure, confusion and other neurological problems.

Did you know?

Cherries, apples and sugar beets also contain small amounts of glycoalkaloids.

The most toxic?

Potato plants produce the most toxic glycoalkaloids found in the edible nightshade family and it is particularly prevalent in potatoes that are green or sprouting. Potatoes have been known to cause livestock deaths by cows and horses feeding on raw potatoes or the plant's foliage. Thankfully, our digestive and immune systems are vastly different.

Autoimmunity and vitamin D

We all know that vitamin D is crucial for proper bone formation. There is, however, a potent form of vitamin D3 in nightshade vegetables that actually prevents proper calcium metabolism. The result is the formation of calcium in the soft tissue rather than in the bones, which is where we need it. This links consumption of nightshades to arthritis and joint pain, especially the autoimmune disease rheumatoid arthritis.

Digestive sensitivity

The symptoms of nightshade intolerance are often confused with intolerance to gluten or dairy, and can include digestive distress, such as bloating, heartburn and IBS, as well as headaches, joint pain or stiffness. Intolerance to nightshades is mostly seen in Caucasians and is mostly genetic. Continuing to eat nightshades while you have an intolerance can increase the risk of developing a 'leaky gut', which causes undigested food particles and bacteria to 'leak' through the intestine and flood directly into the bloodstream due to damage of the small intestine.

If you feel you may have sensitivity to nightshades, you can reduce the effects by peeling your potatoes, avoiding unripe fruit and cooking the vegetable rather than eating it raw.

THE ORCHARD

Fruit trees are an integral part of any productive garden. The post-war immigration era of the 1950s and '60s saw a huge influx of Europeans to countries like Australia, and their legacy can still be found amongst the knotted trunks and fruit of the trees many of us still have in our gardens.

Today, we are quite comfortable with growing our own herbs or veggies in the backyard, but the thought of planting a mini orchard sounds a little more daunting. An orchard doesn't need to be on acreage with row upon row of fruit-bearing trees; three to five beautiful fruit or nut trees will do the trick. For city-dwellers short on space, there are now dwarf options for almost every imaginable variety, and these are perfectly suited for growing in pots and on balconies.

Deciduous orchard trees like apple, plum, pear, cherry and almond trees will change with the seasons, providing beautiful colour and life to your garden or patio throughout the year. Lush green foliage in the summer provides shade for your garden and attracts beneficial insects and pollinators. You'll see brightly coloured leaves through the autumn, then bare winter limbs that burst with stunning blossoms as spring emerges.

With a seasonal supply of quality fresh fruit on hand from your home orchard you are set to produce wonderful dishes and preserves year-round. I adore home-made stewed quinces in autumn; their cooked ruby red fruit is magical. A plum and almond tart or cherry sorbet are impressive desserts that are simple to make. From your apple harvest you can make a simple salad of julienned sweet apples to balance some bitter salad greens, create the iconic French tarte tartin, or even take the time to turn your bounty into home-made apple cider.

When my lemon tree is laden with fruit I love to bottle them up whole with lots of good quality sea salt. Within a month I have home-made preserved lemons that are fantastic stuffed inside roast chicken with fresh thyme, or as a marinade for meaty fish like snapper or rockling. Preserved lemons are also great in Middle Eastern rice dishes, with couscous or in grain-based salads.

Much like any root-to-bloom plant, fruit trees also present opportunities to harvest other parts of the plant besides the fruit. The entire citrus family, for example, has fragrantly-oiled foliage and flowers that can be used to infuse your dishes. Even though the kaffir lime leaf has become the preferred foliage of choice, don't discount the rest of the citrus family.

Many of the leaves, blossoms and woods from the orchard can also be used in cooking. Create a spicy chilli paste with lemon leaves, or harvest orange blossoms before they begin to fruit for home-made orange blossom water. Regular pruning of your fruit trees – which is an essential practice for encouraging better fruit production – results in offcuts that can be used for staking your climbing plant varieties, but these can also be used for smoking.

Cherry

The sight of cherries in the markets signals the arrival of summer and, in Australia, they are an essential Christmas-table centrepiece. The beauty of the cherry far surpasses the scarlet, glossy skins of the fruit. When the tree is in full flower, cherry blossoms are exquisite and a whole tourist trade, called *hanami*, has been formed around the fleeting cherry blossom season in Japan. The two most commonly grown types of cherry are sweet cherry (*Prunus avium*) and sour cherry (*Prunus cerasus*). Part of the rose family, cherries are a stone fruit, or drupe, and are closely related to almonds. They originated in Europe and western Asia and it is believed the Romans discovered the cherry around 70 BC.

Cherries have a short harvest season and require exposure to the cold to germinate. Cherry pits are pre-chilled and planted in autumn, seedlings will emerge in spring and they will not produce fruit until the trees reach three to four years old, achieving full maturity at seven years. Cherry blossoms will appear in mid-spring followed by the peak season of fruit for around a month in the summer.

The fruit and blossoms of the cherry are edible. The Japanese even eat the leaves of some cultivars, including the celebrated sakura cherry blossom, but their sweet and juicy red flesh envelopes a poisonous pit that can cause cyanide poisoning if consumed in large quantities. Surprisingly, despite having a rich red colour that is usually suggestive of a fruit with high nutrient quality, raw sweet cherries provide little nutrients and are 82 per cent water.

This ancient fruit is still celebrated by its European forebears; think black forest cake, kirsch and cerise liqueur.

Apricot

Apricot (*Prunus armeniaca*) is a stone fruit that was originally discovered in the mountainous regions of north-central and north-western China. Over time, the trade routes along the Silk Road spread the fruit from Asia into Europe and, today, most of the apricots found in the New World are of European origin. There are many exotic Moroccan and Persian recipes that use apricots, such as Moroccan tagine with apricots and chicken and the Persian apple and dried apricot stew khoresh sib o gheysi.

In the early stages of spring, edible apricot blossoms precede the small, summer stone fruit. The blossoms, which are usually delicate white clusters of flowers, can be used to garnish both sweet and savoury dishes. Their relatively neutral flavour and soft petals lend them to salads, garnishing desserts such as panna cotta, or apricot-based cocktails.

The sweet summer fruit of the apricot is incredibly versatile. Delicious eaten raw straight from the stone, it can also be dried, pickled, poached, roasted, stuffed, glazed, puréed or steeped. It is a popular ingredient in many dishes, from ethnic cuisines to simple home-made apricot pie or chutney.

In Japan the fruit, wood and flowers are all used to make medicine, treating everything from fever, cough, indigestion and intestinal disorders through to insomnia, easing the symptoms of menopause and in the prevention of cancer and cardiovascular disease.

Spicy apricot chutney

Makes approx. 1 kg (2 lb 3 oz)

This wonderful sweet-and-spicy chutney is made sweet using the natural sugar of the ripe apricots rather than adding refined sugar. It is a fantastic condiment for rice dishes, grilled and barbecued meats, or as a condiment for your cheese platter.

2 red chillies, seeded and diced
2 teaspoons apple-cider vinegar
2 teaspoons white-wine vinegar
650 g (1 lb 7 oz) ripe apricots, stoned and diced
40 g (1½ oz/⅓ cup) raisins
3 cinnamon sticks
pinch of sea salt
4 whole cloves

Combine the chilli and vinegars in a small saucepan and bring to a gentle boil over medium–high heat, then remove from the heat and set aside.

Combine the apricot, raisins, cinnamon sticks, salt and 3 tablespoons water in a saucepan. Set over medium heat and bring to the boil, stirring frequently. Cover, reduce the heat to low, and simmer for about 15 minutes until the fruit has softened and a thick sauce forms.

Stir in the vinegar mixture and whole cloves. Cook for another 2 minutes, stirring frequently, until the mixture is hot. Remove from the heat and cool to room temperature. Discard the cinnamon sticks and whole cloves.

Use immediately or refrigerate for up to 1 week in an airtight container. To store for longer, ladle the hot chutney into sterilised glass jars (see page 14) and seal tightly. The chutney will keep in a cool, dark place, unopened, for 18 months. Once opened, store in the refrigerator for up to 2 months.

Almond

Native to the Middle East, India and North Africa, the almond (*Prunus dulcis*) is most commonly known for its edible seed, and is believed to be one of our oldest cultivated seeds. Part of the rose family, and a cousin of cherries, peaches and plums, almond trees range in size from 6–9 m (19–29 ft) when fully mature.

From early spring, delicate almond blossoms will bloom with a robust sweet aroma reminiscent of jasmine and lily. The blossoms have white/pale pink petals and multiple pollen-laden stamens that, once pollinated, will eventually ripen into the almond fruit. In spring, the fuzzy, greyish-green fruit will form and, by the end of summer, the fruit, or hull, will dry and split open. The almonds are then harvested in late summer to early autumn when the hull and seed dries out and the seed is fully exposed.

Almonds are a true superfood. They contain many healthy fats and are high in protein, magnesium, antioxidants, fibre and vitamin E. Typically regarded as superior to other nuts for their medicinal properties, almonds have also been proven to reduce blood-sugar levels, cholesterol and blood pressure. They can also reduce hunger and promote weight loss.

Two types of almonds are domestically grown: sweet and bitter. The sweet almond is most commonly grown for its nut fruit, while the bitter almond is used as an extract in cosmetics and some foods. It is important to distinguish that, while domesticated almonds are edible, wild almond species are toxic. The fruit of the wild almond contains glycoside amygdalin that, when crushed or chewed, transforms into deadly prussic acid (hydrogen cyanide). All parts of the almond tree contain taxifolin, a natural compound that has anti-tumour properties.

Home-made almond milk

Makes 1 litre (34 fl oz/4 cups)

The recent rise in popularity of almond milk may be due to an increase in gluten intolerance and vegan diets, but there are plenty of good reasons us allergy-free meat eaters should try making our own almond milk. It's low in fat but high in energy, protein and fibre, and also contains calcium, zinc, iron, magnesium and potassium.

Although readily available commercially, there are some benefits to making your own almond milk. Not only is it quick and easy, but home-made almond milk will contain more nuts and less sugar than its commercial counterpart.

Almond milk is also a great substitute for cow's milk as it has a lovely, nutty flavour and creamy texture that's similar to regular milk.

155 g (5½ oz/1 cup) raw organic almonds
875 ml (29½ fl oz/3½ cups) filtered water, plus extra for soaking
½ teaspoon pure vanilla extract
pinch of sea salt
1 tablespoon agave nectar

Put the almonds in a large bowl and cover with cold water. Cover and leave to soak overnight.

Strain the almonds in a colander and leave them to drain for a couple of minutes. Transfer to a food processor and add the filtered water. Blitz at high speed for 2–3 minutes until the almonds are well pulverised. Add the vanilla, salt and agave nectar and pulse to combine.

Line a fine-mesh sieve with muslin (cheesecloth) and strain the almond mixture into a bowl. Squeeze the muslin to extract as much liquid as possible, then discard the solids. Pour the almond milk into a sterilised glass jar or bottle (see page 14) and seal tightly. Refrigerate for up to 3 days, shaking the jar well before each use to mix in the fine sediment.

For different-flavoured almond milks, you can also add vanilla bean paste, cinnamon or chocolate. Just follow the recipe above and add the flavourings just before you transfer the milk to a jar or bottle.

Vanilla-flavoured almond milk
Replace the ½ teaspoon of vanilla extract with 1 tablespoon of pure vanilla bean paste.

Chocolate-flavoured almond milk
Add 1 tablespoon of good-quality cocoa powder before bottling.

Cinnamon-flavoured almond milk
Add 2 whole cinnamon sticks and ¼ teaspoon ground cinnamon to the almond milk and refrigerate for 2 hours before discarding the solids.

WOODS FOR SMOKING

Adding flavour with wood smoke is an ancient and time-honoured method. Smoking meat over a long period of time is also an excellent preservation method. It is important to use woods that are free from resins (sap) and to keep in mind that if you can eat the fruit or nuts of that tree, then the wood is likely to be good (and non-toxic) for smoking.

Here are some examples of good-flavoured woods for smoking:

Almond
A nutty, sweet flavour that is good with all meats.

Apple
Very mild in flavour and gives food sweetness. Good with poultry and pork, but will turn chicken skin dark brown.

Apricot
Great for poultry and pork, with a sweet mild flavour.

Cherry
This is one of the most popular woods for smoking because its sweet, mild flavour goes with almost anything.

Crab apple
Similar to apple wood, with a sweet nutty flavour.

Grapefruit
A mild wood that produces a good, smoky flavour that works with any meat.

Grapevines
A tart-flavoured smoke that can be too heavy for more delicate meats. Use it sparingly with poultry or lamb.

Lemon and orange
A mild wood producing a generous, smoky flavour that will work with most meats.

Mulberry and pear
A sweet flavour that is very similar to apple.

Nectarine and peach
A sweet, mild flavour that is great for poultry and pork.

Pecan
This wood burns quite cool and provides a subtle, delicate flavour.

The best way to use woods for smoking is in chip form. Soak the chips for at least 30 minutes before adding 1–2 handfuls of chips to a smoker box and placing on the grill before adding the meat. Wait until you can actually see the wood smoking, then cook the meat on the grill as required.

SEEDS & PODS

Much like the fruits of summer, the emergence of seed pods from plants such as broad beans and peas is the final act of the cool season. Pods are typically regarded as the plant's first produce but, in fact, they are the last harvest of a plant's production. Most plants that are harvested for their pods are entirely edible and the shoots, leaves and stems can also be eaten.

For millennia, farmers have left crops of peas and beans to dry in the field before being shelled, cleaned and stored for the winter. A rich source of protein, slow-cooked legumes and pulses are a staple in many cuisines, providing sustenance in diets that otherwise might be lacking in valuable nutrients. Pulses are beneficial in the garden too, filling the soil with nitrogen for the incumbent spring plants.

The wonderkid of the bean family, the broad bean, can be harvested for all of its parts, from the root to the seed. Rather than focusing on the mature pods – which often need to be cooked and double-podded – you can use the fresh shoots or foliage in a salad, or its flowers to top canapés. Try blanching the whole baby pods or eating them fresh, like peas.

Using all parts of our seed-producing plants means that we can benefit from interim harvests along the way rather than waiting for the ultimate prize at the end of a long growing season. This not only maximises the plant's yield, but offers new culinary opportunities that go beyond a singular focus on one of its many valuable parts.

BEANS

Fabaceae

Beans are a true all-rounder, both in the kitchen and the garden. Fresh beans and dried beans, or pulses, are a staple in most cuisines for their high levels of protein and other nutrients, and there are hundreds of varieties of dried beans that feature particularly in Middle Eastern, Latin American and Mediterranean diets.

Despite the focus being, well and truly, on their pods and seeds, bean plants produce an abundance of edible foliage that has a slightly nutty flavour and can be used fresh, when young and most palatable, or wilted and sautéed as it matures.

Growing beans in your garden is not only rewarding in a culinary sense, but will provide your soil with extra nutrition for the hungrier crops that follow, such as cool-season brassicas. Dwarf varieties are particularly good for the impatient home gardener, as they yield from 8 weeks onwards, are compact and don't necessarily require trellising. If you are short on space, however, climbing beans are great space-savers. They need a trellis to mount, but will produce more foliage, flowers and, ultimately, beans.

Nutritional value

Beans are a good source of vitamins C and B6, iron, copper, folate, manganese, magnesium, potassium and phosphorus. Both fresh and dried beans are high in protein.

Origin

The oldest-known beans date back to the second millennium BC and were found in the important archaeological site Guitarrero Cave in Peru. However, beans were first domesticated as early as 7,000 BC in the Central American region of Mesoamerica.

Favourite variety

Royal Burgundy, an easy-to-grow dwarf variety that produces the most incredible purple flowers and beans.

Seasonality/In the garden

Beans are a warm-season vegetable that are frost tender. They like well-drained soil with added mulch or compost. As they are prone to fungal diseases, it is important to get your spacing and watering right and to mulch the garden bed well. Soaking the seeds in water prior to planting will speed up their germination and, once plants mature and flowers begin to emerge, a feed of liquid potash will help them set into beans and increase the yield and quality of the produce.

Did you know?

A number of beans, such as raw kidney beans and butter beans, contain the harmful toxin lectin phytohaemagglutinin (or kidney bean lectin), which can poison you. By preparing the beans properly, this toxin is killed off. It involves soaking the beans in water for at least 8 hours, draining them and then boiling in water for at least 10 minutes. In fact, undercooking toxic varieties of beans may be more toxic than eating them in their raw state.

Companion planting

Climbing beans form one part of the 'three sisters' companion planting strategy. Corn is planted first, followed by beans, which provide nitrogen for the corn and, in return, use it as a trellis. Cucumbers then crawl on the soil below, providing pseudo mulching and keeping temperature and moisture consistent.

Pea salad

Serves 2 as a side salad

No parts of the broad bean, coriander or brassica plants should be wasted when they reach the end of their life cycle. These root-to-bloom royals – including peas – can be used for their most tender parts to make up this quick side salad. If you find the foliage and tendrils too tough to be used fresh, consider sautéing with garlic and olive oil for something a little heartier.

40 g (1½ oz/2 cups) pea sprouts
4–5 radishes, thinly sliced on a mandoline
35 g (1¼ oz/¼ cup) feta, crumbled

Dressing
1 tablespoon freshly squeezed lemon juice
1 tablespoon olive oil
1 teaspoon red-wine vinegar
sea salt and freshly ground black pepper

Harvest the pea plants, setting aside the foliage and flowers.
  Toss the pea sprouts and radishes together in a bowl.
  To make the dressing, combine all the ingredients in a bowl and season with salt and pepper to taste. Drizzle over the peas and radishes, and toss to combine.
  Top with crumbled feta to finish.

Garlic and dill fava bean salad

Serves 4–6

This classic Egyptian bean dish has a smoky flavour, complemented nicely by the zest and tang of the fresh herbs, cumin and lemon.

500 g dried fava beans, soaked overnight
60 ml (2 fl oz/¼ cup) olive oil
3 tablespoons chopped fresh flat-leaf (Italian) parsley, plus extra to serve
3 tablespoons chopped fresh dill, plus extra to serve
1 teaspoon ground cumin
4 garlic cloves, mashed into a paste
juice of 1 lemon
sea salt and freshly ground black pepper

Drain the fava beans and put in a saucepan. Cover with water by 10 cm (4 in) and bring to the boil over high heat. Reduce the heat to a simmer, cover, and cook for about 50 minutes, stirring occasionally, until the beans are tender.
  Drain the beans and transfer to a bowl. Add the oil, parsley, dill, cumin, garlic and lemon juice and season with salt and pepper. Leave to sit for 30 minutes to allow the flavours to develop, then serve on a platter garnished with extra parsley and dill.

The fava beans add a good dose of protein and fibre to this satisfying salad (left).

PEAS

Pisum sativum

Fresh peas are always elusive, and it is a rare treat to bring a pea pod fresh, from the garden, to our table. The unsurpassable flavour of freshly-podded peas is like nothing else; delicate, full of natural sugars and rich in flavour. Once the peas have been picked and shucked, their sugars quickly turn to starch and their moment of glory is lost. For this reason, they are best eaten straight away.

High in vitamins A and B, peas are a good source of potassium and calcium and they are considered good for the kidneys and spleen.

Peas have been a staple in our diets since medieval times, making up the classic English dish pease pudding and, in addition to producing a diverse range of varieties for human consumption, they have always fulfilled a couple of useful roles. Growing them has a regenerative effect on our soil as they are full of nitrogen, transferring this to the earth below as they grow. This is why they are commonly used to make Green manure (page 62). In turn, they have become an important livestock food because of the ease with which they produce.

Perhaps it's because we can eat peas straight off the plant that we have been forced to explore its other parts. The wispy tendrils of the plant add a subtle pea flavour to any salad (best dressed with a simple lemon vinaigrette), while the long white stems of the freshly germinated seed are impossibly sweet and tender. Nearing season's end (around the beginning of spring), as we become slightly anxious about planting the warm-blooded crops, it is possible to use the entire plant in our cooking.

If it's the mature podded pea you're after, don't let the casings go to waste. Rather, cut off the tough ends and de-string the fibres along the seams, then use what remains in a stir-fry or soup.

Nutritional value

Peas are a good source of vitamins C, K, B1 and B6, dietary fibre, folate, copper, phosphorus and manganese. They also contain iron, magnesium, potassium, protein and zinc.

Origin

Archaeological discovery of peas dates back as far as the Neolithic period (10,000–2,000 BC) where they were found in Greece, Turkey, Syria and Jordan. They were also present in Egypt, Georgia, Afghanistan, Pakistan and north-west India.

Favourite variety

Sugar Bon sugar snap peas are incredibly sweet and crisp and easy to grow in autumn and spring. It has luscious white flowers with beautiful green veiny detail.

Seasonality/In the garden

Peas are best grown from seed, planted directly into the garden. Wait until the soil temperature begins to drop in autumn, then soak the seeds in water overnight prior to sowing, which will add a reserve of water that speeds up successful germination. They can also be planted in early spring in temperate climates, but do not like summer heat and will flounder in warm weather. Best grown up a trellis, edible pea flowers will be followed by pea pods that can typically be harvested around 60 days after planting. To promote good pod formation, give the plant a feed with potash once it begins to flower, and make sure it collects sufficient sunlight.

BROAD BEAN

Vicia faba

The broad bean is a root-to-bloom A-lister. The entire plant is edible, from its leaves, stem and flowers, all the way to its prized pods, which are typically grown to full size and then double podded. They are, however, palatable at any size and best when young, still nestled in their tender casings. The dried fava bean, a popular legume commonly used in Mediterranean and Moroccan cooking, is another exciting ingredient that comes from the broad bean.

As gardeners, we have always held this plant in high esteem. Part of the legume family, which includes peas and beans, broad beans help to fix our soil stocks with nitrogen that can then be used for subsequent spring crops.

What makes it gardening royalty is its ability to provide a full spectrum of harvesting opportunities then leave its mark on the garden for the greater good. The broad bean truly is a team player.

Nutritional value

Broad beans are high in protein, fibre and potassium as well as vitamins A, B1 and B2. They have no saturated fat or cholesterol.

Origin

Native to North Africa and south-west and south Asia. The oldest-known domesticated beans were found in Guitarrero Cave, an archaeological site in Peru, dating to around the second millennium BC.

Favourite variety

Crimson Red.

Seasonality/In the garden

Broad beans will begin to flower as early as mid-winter, heralding the first signs of spring. Best grown from seed, broad beans can be planted from autumn to early spring, but will perish at the first sign of summer. Keep in mind that the seeds have a 70–90 per cent strike rate, so plant a few in position then thin out the weaker plants when seedlings begin to emerge at 2–4 weeks.

Sweet and crisp broad bean leaf foliage can be picked from about 6 weeks, once the plant has established. Pick sparingly though, so as not to affect the development of the flowers and pods. Since most flowers and pods form on the top half of the plant, picking from the lower segments helps to create good air flow and reduce the potential for pests and diseases.

Pick young, whole broad beans from about week 14, when they are still small and tender (approximately 10 cm/4 in long). Once the pods grow larger, the balance of fluffy casing to pod shifts out of proportion. Larger beans develop an outer skin that some consider tough, but this can be removed.

Broad beans are the ultimate nitrogen fixer, replenishing the soil with this much-needed garden commodity. As production slows and the garden grows impatient for spring, the plant begins to dry out and becomes tough and fibrous. These last limbs should be chopped up and reintegrated back into the soil to maximise the absorption of nitrogen, which will aid subsequent crops.

Best companion plants

Potatoes and sweetcorn.

Broad bean leaf salad

Serves 2

This salad makes a versatile side dish. The sweet, crisp flavour of the broad bean leaves works especially well with gamey meats and crustaceans.

20 g (¾ oz/1 cup) broad bean leaves
50 g (1¾ oz/1 cup) spinach
small handful of fresh flat-leaf (Italian) parsley
small handful of chives
2 spring onions (scallions)

Dressing
½ garlic clove
1 teaspoon dijon mustard
½ tablespoon red-wine vinegar
1½ tablespoons extra-virgin olive oil
1½ tablespoons lemon juice
freshly ground black pepper

Wash and dry the broad bean leaves and spinach, and roughly chop the herbs and spring onions. Combine all the ingredients on a serving platter.

To make the dressing, crush the garlic in a pestle and mortar, then add the dijon mustard. Add the red-wine vinegar, olive oil and lemon juice, and season to taste with pepper. Dress the salad leaves.

Spring vegetable stew

(Vignarola)
Serves 4

3 large globe artichokes
1 kg (2 lb 3 oz) peas in their pods
1 kg (2 lb 3 oz) baby broad beans in their pods
2 large, or 6 small, spring onions (scallions)
6 tablespoons olive oil
1 glass white wine
sea salt

Remove the tough, outer leaves of the artichokes, snapping them off just before the base. Using a sharp knife, pare away the tough outer flesh from the base of the artichokes and the stem. Detach the trimmed stems and slice lengthways into quarters. Cut the trimmed artichoke globes into eight wedges and immerse the wedges and stems in a bowl of acidulated cold water.

Shell the broad beans and peas. If the broad beans are large and have a tough outer coat, remove it by plunging the broad beans into hot water, then in cold water before squeezing the beans out of their coats. Thinly slice the spring onions.

Heat the olive oil in a heavy-based saucepan over medium heat and sauté the spring onion until soft and translucent, then add the artichoke wedges and stems and stir to coat in the oil. Stir in the wine and a pinch of salt, then cover and cook for 15 minutes, stirring from time to time. Add the peas and broad beans, re-cover the pan, and cook for a further 3 minutes. Season to taste with salt. The vignarola is ready when the vegetables are tender. Remove from the heat and leave the stew to sit for a few minutes before serving at room temperature.

Garlic edamame

Serves 4

Edamame beans are immature green soybeans. Originally of Chinese origin, but more commonly associated with Japanese cuisine, edamame beans have risen in popularity over the past decade and are now readily available to purchase frozen from most supermarkets.

400 g (14 oz) fresh or frozen edamame beans in their shells
3 garlic cloves
2 tablespoons olive oil
soy sauce
wasabi paste
sea salt

Bring a large saucepan of salted water to the boil. Add the edamame, bring back to the boil and cook until the beans are bright green, about 3–5 minutes. Drain and set aside.

Crush the garlic cloves with the heavy, flat side of a knife, leaving them whole. Heat the olive oil in a large frying pan, add the garlic and edamame and toss until the outside of the edamame begins to brown slightly.

Transfer to a serving bowl and toss. Serve with a mixture of soy sauce and wasabi paste on the side as a dipping sauce.

If you don't like garlic, coat your edamame (left) in some sweet, sticky miso instead.

NIGELLA

Nigella sativa

One of the oldest known spices, nigella seeds were found
in Tutankhamun's tomb and are mentioned in the Bible's Old
Testament, although their use is not clear. Cultivated and found
growing wild mainly in Egypt and India, they are also native to
other parts of North Africa, western and southern Asia, southern
Europe and the Middle East. The tiny, black, drop-shaped nigella
seeds have a slightly bitter taste with the pungency of onion and
herbaceous notes of oregano. Their pretty blue or white flowers
are also edible and have a neutral flavour, with petals that are
easily separated and can be used on sweet or savoury dishes.

Nigella seeds have something of an identity crisis. They have been referred to as onion seeds, black cumin, black caraway and fennel flower. And, to further confuse things, *Nigella sativa's* close cousin, *Nigella damascena*, or Love-in-the-mist, often tries to take credit for this spice, but its flowers and seeds are merely decorative.

Known simply as nigella (or *kalonji* in Hindi), it is a member of the buttercup (*Ranunculaceae*) family and has been used for thousands of years as a preservative, spice and, as the Prophet Muhammad claimed, a seed with healing powers.

Whatever you may call it, nigella seed is a staple of the spice cabinet in many cultures. In Asia, nigella seeds are used in numerous spice blends, either ground or left whole, and it is widely used in Middle Eastern breads. It is also fantastic in savoury pastries, pilafs, curries, salads, vegetable dishes and pickles, and is a great substitute for sesame seeds.

Nutritional value

Also known as black cumin seed, the oil has been used for centuries in Arabian, African and Asian countries for conditions such as asthma and metabolic syndrome. Today, the oil is extracted, concentrated and sold as gel capsules. It is also a good source of essential fatty acids.

Origin

Native to the Mediterranean region, south and southwest Asia and the Middle East.

Seasonality/In the garden

Nigella is a relatively unfussy annual plant and is a prolific self-seeder. It can grow in either full sun or partial shade and likes a fertile, well-drained soil. It's not recommended to plant nigella in the cooler months as it's prone to powdery mildew and, in the height of summer, it can perish in the heat. When planted regularly or left to self-seed it will yield glorious blue and white flowers for a few weeks from spring to autumn. These flowers are followed by equally beautiful green seed pods. By harvesting the seed pods and hanging them up to dry you can yield your own nigella seeds.

Other facts

Many studies have focused on the chemo-protective properties of plants. Nigella has been shown to have anti-carcinogenic properties in Lewis lung carcinoma; a tumour type discovered by Dr Margaret R. Lewis that is used frequently as a transplantable malignancy in studies with mice.

Traditional uses for nigella seed in different cultures

Preserved lemons in Morocco
Naan bread in India
Korma in India
String cheese in the Middle East
Potato stir-fry in Bengal

SKINCARE

These days, it seems like every moisturiser, cleanser and anti-aging product at the beauty counter claims to be packed with exotic natural plant extracts and ingredients. The reality is, these botanical extracts are used in very small amounts and have, in fact, been stabilised with a potion of synthetics, preservatives, sulphates and acids.

Many plants, herbs and flowers can be easily grown in your garden and used to form a home-made beauty cabinet and first-aid kit. In fact, you are probably growing a number of them already. Some plants are great at soothing irritated skin, others at moisturising, and some even treat acne.

Calendula petals soothe the skin, reduce inflammation and heal burns, sunburn, acne, eczema and skin abrasions. They can also be used fresh or dried in different recipes, such as healing balms, toners, moisturisers and tinctures. The gel inside aloe vera leaves can be used straight, without any processing, to soothe and heal sunburned and inflamed skin, or it can be added to moisturising lotions. The puréed flesh of cucumber can be used for making face masks, and rose petals picked fresh from your garden make a wonderful natural skin toner.

Fresh yarrow leaves have incredible healing powers; by simply rubbing onto cuts, they will induce clotting to stop bleeding and are very effective for skin irritations such as insect bites, nappy rash and burns. Green tea, which is most commonly consumed for its antioxidant properties, will improve the condition of aging skin and has been shown to control oil production (causing acne), bacterial growth and to reduce inflammation.

Scientists conducted a study that showed thyme infused in a tincture (herb macerated in alcohol) was more effective at clearing acne than treatments using benzoyl peroxide. Rosewater is a mild astringent and toner especially good for mature skin, but can be used on all skin types. It helps cleanse and tone while boosting cell regeneration and moisture levels.

Yarrow first-aid balm

Makes 250 ml (8½ fl oz/1 cup)

Yarrow is the go-to natural remedy for topical first-aid needs. It's also really easy to grow and can readily be found growing wild. It is such a versatile herb with so many different medicinal properties. Yarrow contains achilletin and achilleine to stimulate clotting in cuts and abrasions, it works wonders on itchy skin rashes and bites, and has also been shown to have sedative, pain-killing, antiseptic, anti-inflammatory and antispasmodic properties.

Here's a list of things medicinal yarrow balm can be used for:

Bee stings

Bleeding from minor cuts

Scrapes

Burns

Rashes

Headaches

Insect bites

Nappy rash

250 ml (8½ fl oz/1 cup) Yarrow-
  infused oil (see below)
30 g (1 oz) beeswax, broken into
  small pieces

Yarrow-infused oil

20–40 g (¾ –1½ oz/1–2 cups)
  freshly harvested yarrow leaves
  and/or flowers (if they have any
  moisture on them, let them dry
  out for a day before using)
olive oil

To make the yarrow-infused oil, roughly chop the yarrow leaves and pack into a sterilised glass jar (see page 14). Pour in enough olive oil to completely immerse the leaves, then seal the jar tightly and leave in a cool, dark place for 3–4 weeks to macerate.

Strain the mixture through a fine-mesh sieve or muslin (cheesecloth), discarding the leaves. Store the yarrow oil in a sterilised glass jar out of direct sunlight.

To make the balm, combine the yarrow oil and beeswax in a glass jar. Place the jar in the top half of a double boiler and add 5–10 cm (2–4 in) water in the bottom. Set the pan over a medium–low heat and heat gently until the beeswax has melted.

Carefully pour the balm into sterilised 500 ml (17 fl oz/2 cup) glass jars (see page 14) and seal tightly (dark-coloured jars are ideal as they will protect the balm from light). The balm can be stored in a cool, dark place at room temperature for 6–12 months before it begins to lose its potency.

Like all herbal products, make sure you test a small patch of the balm on your skin before use to ensure you don't have an allergic reaction. It has been said that pregnant women should not use yarrow.

Note: This method of making infused oil needs to be started well in advance, however you can make a warm infused oil in 2 hours by following the method for Warm oil infusion on page 200.

Calendula and honey body lotion

Makes approx. 200 ml (7 fl oz)

35 g (1¼ oz) Calendula-infused
  sweet almond oil (see below)
20 g (¾ oz) emulsifying wax
140 g (5 oz) Oat-infused water
  (see below)
5 g (¼ oz) honey
2 g (²⁄₈ oz) vitamin E oil
20 drops rose geranium essential oil
  (optional)
broad-spectrum, water-soluble
preservative, such as liquid Germall
Plus, which is used to inhibit the
growth of bacteria and mould
in cosmetic products (optional)

Calendula-infused sweet almond oil

250 g (9 oz) dried calendula petals
  (see page 167)
750 ml (25½ fl oz/3 cups) sweet
  almond oil or olive, sunflower
  or good-quality vegetable oil

Oat-infused water

Makes 250 ml (8½ fl oz/1 cup)

1 teaspoon oats
250 ml (8½ fl oz/1 cup) boiling
  distilled water

You will need:
Heatproof bowls and containers
Hand-held milk frother
Digital thermometer

To make the calendula almond oil, combine the dried calendula petals with the cold oil in the bowl of a double boiler. Place over simmering water and simmer for 2 hours, topping up the water if necessary. Remove from the heat and leave the oil to cool to room temperature.

Line a fine-mesh sieve with muslin (cheesecloth) and suspend over a clean bowl. Strain the oil, discarding the petals. Set aside.

For the oat-infused water, put the oats in a bowl and pour over the boiling water. Allow to sit for a few minutes, then strain the liquid into a jug, discarding the oats. Weigh 140 g (5 oz) of the water and keep warm – around 66°C/150°F – until needed.

To make the lotion, combine the oil and emulsifying wax in a double boiler and melt. Once melted, measure the temperature with the thermometer. The ingredients need to be around 66°C/150°F.

Once the oil and water are at the right temperature, submerge the milk frother in the water and slowly trickle in the oil. Without turning the frother on, gently stir the ingredients then turn it on and blend the lotion for about 30 seconds until it thickens slightly. Keep the head of the frother completely submerged to avoid air bubbles and foam in your lotion. Set the lotion aside to cool.

When the lotion has cooled to about 45°C (113°F), stir in the honey, vitamin E oil, and rose geranium oil and water-soluble preservative, if using. If using a specific preservative, follow the manufacturer's instructions.

Once combined, spoon the cream into an airtight container. If you haven't used a preservative, use the lotion within 1 week. A preservative can extend the shelf-life for 18 months or longer.

Non-toxic sunscreen
Makes 325 ml (11 fl oz)

You can add essential oils, such as lavender oil or vanilla extract, to this sunscreen. Just be sure not to use citrus essential oils as they increase sun sensitivity.

The beeswax will determine the thickness of this sunscreen. For thicker sunscreen add more, for smooth sunscreen add less.

125 ml (4 fl oz/½ cup) almond or olive oil
125 ml (4 fl oz/½ cup) coconut oil
110 g (4 oz/¼ cup) beeswax
1 teaspoon red raspberry seed oil or carrot seed oil
2 tablespoons shea butter
2 tablespoons zinc oxide

Combine all the ingredients except the zinc oxide in a sterilised 500 ml (17 fl oz/2 cup) glass jar (see page 14).

Place the jar in a saucepan with 5 cm (2 in) water in the base. Loosely screw the lid on the jar and place the saucepan over medium heat. As the water heats, the ingredients in the jar will melt and emulsify. Stir occasionally to combine.

Once melted, stir in the zinc oxide. It is important to wear a mask when handling the zinc oxide to avoid inhaling it.

Remove from the heat and carefully pour the sunscreen into a clean sterilised glass jar or container. Avoid using a pump bottle and, instead, apply the sunscreen like body butter. It is best stored at room temperature.

This sunscreen is not waterproof and will need to be reapplied after sweating or swimming.

Note: Many of the ingredients in this recipe have a natural SPF (sun protection factor). This is a natural recipe that has not been tested by a regulatory organisation for exact SPF, so it's unknown what the combined SPF of this sunscreen is. Below is a list of the SPF of some of these natural ingredients:

Almond oil: SPF 5

Coconut oil: SPF 4–6

Zinc oxide: SPF 2–20, depending on how much is used

Red raspberry seed oil: SPF 25–50

Carrot seed oil: SPF 35–40

Shea butter: SPF 4–6

Lemon and thyme salt scrub

Makes 250 ml (8½ fl oz/1 cup)

This face and body scrub is packed with all kinds of natural goodness! Salt is an amazing natural exfoliator, detoxifier and antiseptic agent, while sweet almond oil adds moisture and smells incredible. Lemon is a well-known hero of the natural skincare world. It is great for treating pigmentation problems, acne and softening your skin. Thyme also acts as a natural astringent for your skin and contains plenty of antioxidants.

This scrub is incredibly simple to make. All you need is a clean jar with an airtight lid and, in a few minutes, you'll have your own natural non-toxic scrub.

Before each use just give the scrub a stir to mix the oil and salt back together. Apply to your face and body in gentle, circular motions, rinse with warm water, and your skin will be hydrated and exfoliated.

315 g (11 oz/1 cup) sea salt
125 ml (4 fl oz/½ cup) pure organic
    almond oil
zest of 1 lemon
2 teaspoons thyme leaves

Put the salt in a clean, sterilised glass jar or container (see page 14) with a tight-fitting lid. Add the lemon zest and thyme and pour the almond oil over top. Stir to combine well and seal tightly.

The scrub will keep for up to 6 months in an airtight container at room temperature.

Try adding some essential oils to this scrub (left). Tea tree oil is great for drawing out impurities in the skin and lavender oil is a relaxant.

OIL INFUSIONS

Oil infusions can be used in creams and lotions, but they're especially good for making waterless products such as balms, ointments and massage oils. Many of the beneficial components of medicinal flowers and plants are oil-soluble, meaning that instead of infusing them in water, you can infuse them in oil.

Most herbs and plants in skincare products are used in dried or powdered form, particularly the roots of a plant. It's also best to dry your herbs and flowers before using them in oil infusions if you intend to use the infusions in waterless products without preservatives.

Oil infusions are suitable for herbs and flower petals with a low water content. Dried and powdered roots work too.

Cold oil infusion

Makes 750 ml (25½ fl oz/3 cups)

250 g (9 oz) dried botanicals, such as calendula, chamomile, ginger, lavender and lemon balm
750 ml (25½ fl oz/3 cups) good-quality olive oil, sweet almond oil or sunflower oil

Place the dried botanicals in a sterilised glass jar (see page 14) and cover with oil. Store the jar on a sunny window ledge for at least 1 week and up to 4 weeks, shaking once a day. After 1 week, the infusion can be stored in a cool, dry place for up to 1 year.

Warm oil infusion

Makes 750 ml (25½ fl oz/3 cups)

250 g (9 oz) dried botanicals, such as calendula, chamomile, ginger, lavender and lemon balm
750 ml (25½ fl oz/3 cups) good-quality olive oil, sweet almond oil or sunflower oil

Combine the dried botanicals and oil in the top half of a double boiler and fill the bottom half with water. Place the pan over medium heat and simmer gently for 2 hours, topping up the water if necessary. Remove from the heat and leave the oil to cool completely.
  Line a fine-mesh sieve with a piece of muslin (cheesecloth) and strain the oil into a sterilised glass jar (see page 14), discarding the botanicals.
  Store in a cool, dry place for up to 1 year.

WATER INFUSIONS

A water infusion is essentially a tea. It is suitable for most flower petals and herbs, and can be used in creams, lotions and rinses, or on its own as a toner. Water infusions don't last very long, but you can refrigerate them for 2–3 days.

You can either dry botanicals by air-drying (see page 167), in a solar or electric dehydrator, or in the oven at a very low temperature. Flower petals and thin leaves will take less than an hour to dry in the oven or dehydrator, but fruit, thick leaves and roots will take much longer (up to a few days) depending on what you are drying.

Water infusion

Makes 250 ml (8½ fl oz/1 cup)

1 teaspoon dried botanicals, or
  2 teaspoons fresh botanicals,
  such as calendula, rose petals
  or yarrow leaves
250 ml (8½ fl oz/1 cup) boiling
  distilled water

Put the dried botanicals in a bowl and pour over the boiling water. Leave to infuse for 15–20 minutes, then strain the liquid into a sterilised glass jar (see page 14), discarding the botanicals. Leave to cool completely, then seal the jar tightly.

The water infusion is now ready to use in creams, lotions, rinses or on its own as a toner.

About the authors

Jocelyn Cross

For Jocelyn, both the kitchen and garden are places of contemplation and pleasure – they're not about the work that's involved, but a place to be creative and resourceful.

Jocelyn spent her childhood on a cattle farm in Buxton, Central Victoria, where her frugal mother made the most of everything on the land, from the blackberries that grew as noxious weeds, to the productive veggie garden, an orchard and their own beef and laying chickens. To Jocelyn's family, understanding the provenance of their food was a necessity rather than a mindful way of life.

After working for 15 years as an interior designer, Jocelyn decided to return to her farming roots on a whim and began Petite Ingredient, an organic edible flower business, in a large greenhouse in the Yarra Valley in regional Victoria. In the seven years since its inception, Petite Ingredient has grown to become the most sought-after edible flower brand, supplying Australia and Asia's best chefs.

This is Jocelyn's first book.

Mat Pember

Mat Pember is Australia's best-selling gardening author and founder of Melbourne-based business, Little Veggie Patch Co. After studying Commerce at University of Melbourne, he headed overseas to realise a love for all things food and gardening, coming back to set up the business in 2008. He is a father of two girls, Emiliana and Marlowe, and now lives in a city apartment, where he and his girls make the most of every single plant while strictly controlling the caterpillar population. He is motivated by food, family and thoughtful living, and is still trying to strike a balance between an efficient city life and a more rambling country existence. He hopes that, one day soon, developers will start building more than just structures, and cities will be full of rooftop gardens and neighbours comparing the size of their cucumbers and heat of their chillies.

Acknowledgements

Jocelyn Cross

To my mother, who inspired my love of plants, and to my darling dad who passed away just before this book went to print. To my kind friends and family who fed me and cared for Harry while I simultaneously wrote this book and battled through breast cancer treatment.

I would like to thank Jane Willson and the Hardie Grant team for being so incredibly enthusiastic about our idea from day one. Jane, you had such faith in this book from the beginning and have been very supportive to me as a first-time author. Thank you to our editor, Andrea O'Connor, you are not only patient and precise, but a damn good cook and one cool chick. To our creative team, Bonnie Savage, Leesa O'Reilly and Vaughan Mossop, thank you for all the laughs and good conversation during long days of shooting, but, most of all, thank you for making *Root to Bloom* such a beautiful book.

Lastly, thank you to my friend and co-author, Mat. It was over many glasses of red at Enoteca and phone conversations on my lonely drive up to the farm that the idea of the root-to-bloom food movement was born. It has been a delight working with you; your energy and cheeky nature has always kept things fun and interesting.

Mat Pember

There's always so many good people that go into making a book, and there's no exception here. Starting at the beginning, thanks to Jane Willson and the team at Hardie Grant for having faith (some may call it blind) in our idea and giving us the opportunity to put it on shelves. To Andrea O'Connor, our leader and editor, and the person that wore so many hats on this book she could barely see daylight come the end. For being calm and concise as always, and for taking the leap into the freelance world. Welcome to the life of the home office! Thanks, Vaughan Mossop, for making *Root to Bloom* so earthy and edible, and to Bonnie Savage for capturing it. Thanks to Leesa O'Reilly for making the food look so good.

Sometimes you hope a book drags out for more opportunities to forage perfectly formed weeds and gnarly-looking carrots, but you were just too proficient. To my sister, Elise Heslop, for lending out her studio space and allowing us to farm kohlrabi within it. And, as always, to my girls, Emi and Marlowe, who I hope will always squish caterpillars between their fingers, and my Mum and Dad for the opportunities they continue to give me.

Index

Published in 2018 by Hardie Grant Books,
an imprint of Hardie Grant Publishing

Hardie Grant Books (Melbourne)
Building 1, 658 Church Street
Richmond, Victoria 3121

Hardie Grant Books (London)
5th & 6th Floors
52–54 Southwark Street
London SE1 1UN

hardiegrantbooks.com

A catalogue record for this
book is available from the
National Library of Australia

Root to Bloom
978 1 74379 344 2

10 9 8 7 6 5 4 3 2

Publishing Director: Jane Willson
Project Editor & Editor: Andrea O'Connor @ Asterisk & Octopus
Design Manager: Jessica Lowe
Designer: Vaughan Mossop @ Neighbourhood Creative
Photographer: Bonnie Savage
Stylist: Leesa O'Reilly
Production Manager: Todd Rechner

Colour reproduction by Splitting Image Colour Studio.
Printed in China by Leo Paper Product. LTD.